The New Bitcoin Revolution!

Discover How to Trade Your Way to Riches During the 2021 Bull Run! Futures, Options and Swing Trading Explained Step by Step!

work can be in any fashion deemed liable for any hardship or damages that may befall them after undertaking information described herein.

Additionally, the information in the following pages is intended only for informational purposes and should thus be thought of as universal. As befitting its nature, it is presented without assurance regarding its prolonged validity or interim quality. Trademarks that are mentioned are done without written consent and can in no way be considered an endorsement from the trademark holder.

Charles Swing & Masaru Nakamoto

Bitcoin Revolution

The Ultimate Bitcoin and Blockchain Guide to Master the World of Cryptocurrency and Take Advantage of the 2021 Bull Run!

work can be in any fashion deemed liable for any hardship or damages that may befall them after undertaking information described herein.

Additionally, the information in the following pages is intended only for informational purposes and should thus be thought of as universal. As befitting its nature, it is presented without assurance regarding its prolonged validity or interim quality. Trademarks that are mentioned are done without written consent and can in no way be considered an endorsement from the trademark holder.

Table of Contents

Bitcoin

Introduction

B itcoin has taken the world by storm once again when it crossed $20,000 per BTC in December of last year. After more than 2 years of bear market, the most famous cryptocurrency surpassed its previous all time high.

A lot of people are now trying to improvise themselves as professional investors and are losing a lot of money, only helping those who actually know what they are doing accumulate an incredible amount of wealth that will lead to generational fortunes.

To join the club of the few investors that actually make it, you need the right strategies and the right mindset. Notice how we did not include a large initial capital. In fact, while having more money to trade with means having more fire power, it is not necessary to have thousands of dollars to accumulate Bitcoin and build wealth.

In fact, when we started investing in Bitcoin we only had a few hundreds to put into the market, but that sum yielded us thousands and thousands of dollars over the span of a few years.

Bitcoin

In this book you are going to discover all the strategies that have allowed us to take investing skills to the next level and everything that helped us understand Bitcoin. If you diligently apply our advice, we are sure you are going to see amazing results in a relative short period of time, since this bull run is offering an amazing number of opportunities.

Please, stay away from all the shiny objects of the cryptocurrency world. Just focus on Bitcoin, study it deeply and then milk it like a cash cow!

To your success!

Charles Swing and *Masaru Nakamoto*

Chapter 1 - What is Bitcoin?

Bitcoin (฿, BTC, XBT) is a cryptocurrency otherwise called cryptographic currency. In the case of the unitary denomination, it is written "bitcoin" and, in the case of the peer-to-peer payment system, it is written "Bitcoin". The idea was first presented in November 2008 by one person, or a group of people, under the pseudonym Satoshi Nakamoto. The source code for the implementation of Bitcoin was released in 2009.

The G20 considers Bitcoin to be a "crypto-asset". The term "crypto-asset" refers to "virtual assets stored on an electronic wallet allowing a community of users accepting them in payment to carry out transactions without having to resort to legal tender".

Operation

To create and manage bitcoins, Bitcoin relies on software. In this software, bitcoins are created according to a protocol that pays the agents (called "miners") who have processed transactions. These agents use their computing power to verify, secure and record the transactions in a virtual ledger called the blockchain. The word blockchain comes from the fact that the basic entity of Bitcoin is called a block, and that the blocks are then connected in a chain.

For each new block accepted, the verification-security-recording activity, called mining, is remunerated by newly created bitcoins and by the costs of the transactions processed. As a currency or a commodity, bitcoin can be exchanged for other currencies or commodities, goods or services. The cryptocurrency exchange rate is set on specialized marketplaces and fluctuates according to the law of supply and demand.

It is possible to buy bitcoins online on specialized platforms, physical terminals or in exchange for any good or service with a person who already has them (the transaction can be done from smartphone to smartphone). The platforms also make it possible to follow in real time the evolution of the price of bitcoin compared to other currencies or cryptocurrencies.

Account unit

Bitcoin's unit of account is bitcoin. Its emission is limited to 20,999,999.977 units, each divisible to the eighth decimal place (called Satoshi or Sat). The official currency symbol was registered and accepted in 2015 with Unicode. The corresponding acronyms, used by the exchange platforms, are BTC and XBT. Among the unofficial symbols used are ฿ and Ƀ.

Decentralization

The system operates without a central authority or a single administrator. It is managed in a decentralized manner thanks to the consensus of all the nodes of the network. Bitcoin is the largest decentralized crypto currency, with a capitalization of over one trillion dollars as of April 5th, 2021 ($ 130 billion as of January 1st, 2020).

Means of payment

As a means of payment, bitcoin is accepted by a growing number of merchants, encouraged by transaction fees generally lower than the 2 to 3% charged by credit card organizations and independent of the amount of the financial transaction. However, in 2017 the fees increased dramatically over the

14

course of a few months, from $0.2 in 2016 to $20 on certain days in December 2017, so that the Steam platform or Microsoft withdrew Bitcoin as a payment method, precisely because of too high transaction fees (Microsoft again authorized Bitcoin in January 2018).

In order to address the issue of excessively high transaction fees, the gradual rollout of various technology enhancements (Segwit, Lightning Network, batch transactions, Schnorr) throughout 2018 and 2019 allowed fees to drop to around $0.05 for non-urgent transactions, and even amounts less than $ 0.0001 for Lightning type transactions. Unlike credit cards, any charges are borne not by the seller but by the buyer, who chooses to pay them voluntarily. A bitcoin transaction is irrevocable and cannot be reversed. Despite a 500% growth in the number of merchants accepting bitcoin in 2014, the cryptocurrency is not very established in the retail trade, but continues to gain a foothold in trade.

Use

Between January 2009 and March 2010, using bitcoin was a hobby among crypto enthusiasts, and bitcoin had no real value. However, in April 2010, bitcoin started trading in an exchange for $0.003, and soon after, in May 2010, it was already worth $0.01. A few months later, in July 2010, 0.08 dollars were added to its value again. These numbers reflect the rapid rise in prices that this zero-value cryptocurrency has experienced at 10 cents.

Since its creation in 2009 and until the closure by the American authorities of Silk Road in 2013, bitcoin was used mainly as a medium of exchange by criminal networks for gambling, the purchase of illicit substances, or for hacked databases. The cryptocurrency has attracted the attention of financial authorities, legislative bodies in various countries, particularly the United States, and the mainstream media.

Nevertheless, in recent years, cryptocurrency has matured and a growing number of studies conclude that these illegal activities, although they still exist as in any payment system, only involve a minority share of cryptocurrency exchanges. The United States Senate also recognizes that bitcoin makes it possible to provide perfectly legitimate financial services.

Safe store of value

According to some of the experts, bitcoin would be a safe haven much more than a means of payment, even if unlike gold, Bitcoin can indeed be used for these two purposes. Conversely, other financial experts consider Bitcoin to be far too volatile to be a safe haven, but it has only existed since 2009 and its possible safe haven status will only be possible after a first period of intense volatility . As for the question of whether Bitcoin can reach the market value of gold (or even exceed it), this remains much debated. However, it should be noted that with its trillion dollars evaluation, Bitcoin is not too far from reaching the value of Silver, which is approximately 1.4 trillion dollars.

Chapter 2 - The History of Bitcoin

Bitcoin is an improvement on the concept of b-money, imagined by Wei Dai in 1999, and bitgold, described in 2005 by Nick Szabo. Bitcoin in particular solves the crucial problem of the trust model: servers considered serious vote with their computing power to determine the legitimate transaction chain. In b-money, the servers were supposed to pay a security deposit according to a not very explicit mechanism. The idea of using a computational proof chain was put forward in the bitgold project although Nick Szabo only proposed to use a majority of addresses to establish the legitimacy of a chain of transactions, which left the problem of controlling the number of addresses.

Satoshi Nakamoto claimed that he worked on bitcoin from 2007 to 2009. As early as 2008, he posted a document on a mailing list describing the digital currency. In February 2009, he published an announcement about his work on the P2P Foundation site. On January 3, 2009, the first block or genesis block was created. In February 2009, he distributed the first version of the Bitcoin software on the P2P Foundation site and to operate the network, he used his computer and thus generated the first bitcoins. Along with other developers, Nakamoto continued the implementation of the software and its Bitcoin-Qt version until 2010.

Developers and the bitcoin community gradually lost contact with him in the middle of 2010. On December 12, 2010, a final message was posted by Nakamoto on the main forum. Shortly before disappearing, Nakamoto designates Gavin Andresen as his successor by giving him access to the SourceForge bitcoin project and a copy of the alert key. The latter is a unique private cryptographic key allowing to mitigate the effects of a potential attack on the Bitcoin system, such as the discovery of a cryptographic flaw allowing to modify the transactions, or the take of control of more than 51% of the nodes in the network. During an alert, the operators of the nodes of the network can either warn their users or stop recording transactions.

On September 27, 2012, the Bitcoin Foundation was created. Important characters from the world of new technologies quickly supported the project, such as Wences Casares.

The identity of Satoshi Nakamoto

Several people claimed to be Satoshi Nakamoto, but none of them could prove it. There is no trace of his identity before the creation of Bitcoin. On his profile, Satoshi claimed to be a 40-year-old Japanese.

In March 2014, journalist Leah McGrath Goodman from Newsweek magazine announced that she had tracked down the inventor of Bitcoin who she said would be a 64-year-old Japanese-American whose birth name is "Satoshi Nakamoto", although he changed his name to "Dorian Prentice Satoshi Nakamoto" at the age of 23. He is believed to be a retired physicist living in California. This thesis was methodically dismantled a month later by linguists from Aston University in England who carried out an in-depth study of the linguistic correspondences between the written productions of the author of the Bitcoin white paper and several suspected personalities, notably Dorian Nakamoto.

In 2016, Craig Steven Wright, an Australian entrepreneur, claimed to be Satoshi Nakamoto. However, strong doubts remain.

Adoption

The history of Bitcoin adoption is quite remarkable, as it has been a long process of fake bans and unjustified threats to the cryptocurrency space. In the following pages we are going to track back the adoption process of Bitcoin, starting from 2012. Here are the main milestones of BTC adoption.

- On November 16th, 2012, WordPress started accepting bitcoins for its paid services.

- On November 28th, 2012, the remuneration of miners decreased for the first time, from 50 to 25 BTC. The bitcoin source code provides for a halving of the remuneration every two hundred and ten thousand blocks mined, or approximately every four years.

- On December 6th, 2012, a partnership between the startup Paymium (French exchange site) and the company Aqoba (payment institution) enabled Paymium to operate as a payment service provider, and therefore to keep accounts in euros and issue payment cards usable in euros and bitcoins. On February 14th, 2013, the Reddit community site set up a system to buy "Reddit Gold" with bitcoins.

- On February 16th, 2013, the online storage site Mega, successor to Megaupload, started accepting payments in bitcoin. On October 14th, 2013, the giant Baidu (Chinese equivalent of Google) started accepting bitcoin transactions for its Jiasule firewall service.

- On October 29th, 2013, the first automatic bitcoin cash dispenser-exchanger went into service in Vancouver. In September 2016, more than seven hundred and seventy of these automatic distributor-exchangers were installed worldwide, including four in France.

- On November 21st, 2013, the University of Nicosia announced that it accepted bitcoin and opened a master's degree in economics specializing in digital currencies. On November 22nd, 2013, Richard Branson announced that Virgin Galactic was going to accept bitcoins as a means of payment for its space tourism flights.

- On November 29th, 2013, Jiangsu Telecom (third largest Chinese operator), a subsidiary of China Telecom, started accepting bitcoins.

- On March 25th, 2014, the US tax authorities declared that bitcoin should not be considered as a currency, but as a commodity, whose transactions are subject to taxation on capital gains. This involves taking into account the exchange rate at which a bitcoin has been acquired and the one at which it is used in order to calculate the realized gain, which makes the legal use of bitcoin in the United States particularly difficult.

- On May 9th, 2014, the United States Election Commission accepted that election campaigns could be funded in bitcoins up to a limit of $100 per election cycle.

- On September 23rd, 2014, Paypal allowed certain North American digital goods merchants selected by partner bitcoin payment processors to accept payments in bitcoins, and thus very gradually opened up to bitcoin. As of October 16th, 2017, there were Bitcoin ATMs around the world.

- In December 2017, the French Minister of Public Accounts, Gérald Darmanin, reminded French taxpayers of the requirement to declare income, when it comes to capital gains realized during bitcoin transactions.

- In November 2018, the Ohio government announced that it was accepting Bitcoin tax payments. In January 2020, an investing.com study revealed that 9% of financial advisers already put part of their client's funds in bitcoin to protect them from monetary troubles.

Important moments

During the adoption phase there have been quite a few important moments that changed the course of Bitcoin's life. Here are the most important ones.

- On August 15th, 2010, a block was generated containing a transaction creating 184,467,440,737 bitcoins for three different addresses. This flaw is linked to the fact that the code did not foresee the case of creating such large amounts of bitcoins. This problem was solved automatically by the bitcoin blockchain and these bitcoins no longer exist.

- On March 12th, 2013, an incident occurred related to the non-backward compatibility of version 0.8.0: the chain split into several versions and some remained blocked for a few hours. After a few moments of panic, the system was able to correct itself, signaling the strength of the blockchain technology.

- On April 11th, 2013, the value of bitcoin collapsed from $266 to $105 before stabilizing at $160 in less than six hours. On April 13th, the price reached $66. This massive drop occurred after a big bull run, where the price of Bitcoin rose six times in just a few weeks. For those that are already familiar with Bitcoin's price action, we are sure they are smiling just by thinking about such low prices.

- On October 2nd, 2013, Ross Ulbricht was arrested. He was the alleged founder of Silk Road, which was shut down by the FBI and used only bitcoin for all of its transactions. More on that in a dedicated chapter.

- On February 11th, 2014, the Bitcoin network was the victim of a massive and concerted attack launched on numerous exchange platforms, where quite a few bitcoins were stolen. This was just the preview of what was going to happen a few days later. In fact, on February 24th, 2014, the Mt. Gox trading platform suffered a record loss of 744,408 BTC, the equivalent of more than 44 billion dollars. The site was closed shortly after. A crisis management document has been drawn up and is publicly available on its website, we suggest you check it out because it is quite interesting (https://www.mtgox.com/). Due to this incident, bitcoin lost more than 38% of its value in the first quarter of 2014. On September 11th, 2015, Mark Karpelès, owner of the Mt. Gox platform was indicted in Japan for embezzlement. He is suspected of having embezzled 2.3 million dollars of bitcoin deposits.

- In May 2016, the Gatecoin exchange site was hacked and had 250 bitcoins and 185,000 ether stolen. The hacker managed to bypass the online storage limits of the exchange platform's assets: while only 5% of the deposits are not cold stored, the hacker managed to empty these deposits while continuing to feed the address by transfer of cold storage assets from the exchange platform. After this event, almost every trading and exchanging platform decided to implement a new protection mechanism, in order to improve their safety.

- On August 3rd, 2016, the Bitfinex exchange site reported the theft of 119,756 bitcoins on its exchange platform, which at the time counted for around $65 million.

- On May 7th, 2019, hackers stole more than 7,000 Bitcoins from the Binance Cryptocurrency Exchange, worth over US $40 million. Binance CEO Zhao Changpeng said, "Hackers used a variety of techniques, including phishing, viruses and other attacks. They had the patience to wait and perform well orchestrated actions through multiple independent accounts at the most opportune moment". It was this event that inspired Binance to improve its protection mechanism even further.

All incidents related to exchange platforms only affect people who do not themselves hold the private keys of their bitcoin wallet. Not your keys, not your bitcoins as they say. As you can see, every time the Bitcoin network has been attacked, new solutions were found to make sure the same issue would not happen in the future. In our opinion, this is one of the main strengths in this system. In fact, since it is developed by people, it can easily adapt to new hacking methods and attacks. It is pretty interesting to see the evolution of Bitcoin and if you want to actually invest in it safely, you need to know a bit of its history as well.

A common hacking technique

The technique known as the Trojan Horse makes it possible to change the address of the recipient of the cryptocurrency transaction. CryptoShuffler is one of the software using this technique. This rare technique has little effect because it suffices for the payment sender to visually check the first/last characters of the destination address to make sure that it is not being fooled.

Price evolution against the dollar

When it was created in February 2009, the cryptocurrency was initially traded only as an experiment by a few rare users and its value was zero. On October 12th, 2009, the first known bitcoin sale took place, where two users traded 5,050 bitcoins for $5.02 using a Paypal transfer, which equates to a price of around $0.001 per bitcoin.

In March 2010, Bitcoinmarket.com was the first bitcoin exchange platform to be opened, thus allowing continuous quotation of the price of bitcoin. It was the beginning of an era and every Bitcoin enthusiast should be thankful to this website for what it has done for the community.

On February 9th, 2011, bitcoin reached the valuation of one full dollar. On November 29th, 2013, the value of a bitcoin exceeded that of an ounce of gold, to nearly $1,250. Once again, for those that are familiar with today price action, these numbers do not seem so incredible. However, if you think about it, we are talking about a huge price development in just a couple of years. What other asset did over 1000% in just two years? The answer is very simple: no other asset managed to do it.

Bitcoin, mainly traded for yuan and dollars, can also be traded for euros on a dozen platforms. Until November 2013, Mt. Gox was the most important of these platforms in terms of transaction volume (~ 70%) and the practice had been taken to consider its price as representative of the market. As a result of the problems encountered, users turned away from it, causing the price of bitcoin to drop sharply on Mt. Gox, with prices observed on other platforms only slightly affected.

The price experienced a 400% increase between January and March 2013, before correcting itself severely on April 10th, following a failure of the Mt. Gox exchange site and probable panic sales. The price fell back to the level of the previous month, around $50. Between December 4th and 5th, 2013, following a warning from the People's Bank of China and the Bank of France, the price lost nearly 35% in 24 hours.

On February 19th, 2014, the price collapsed following the announcement of the disappearance of 850,000 bitcoins on Mt. Gox. On this exchange platform, bitcoin goes from $185, on February 18, to $73 24 hours later, while it remains close to $400 on other platforms. Mt.Gox declared bankruptcy on February 28, 2014. On May 1st, 2014, a group of investors by the name of Sunlot Holdings offered to buy the site for one symbolic bitcoin.

In 2016, after the Brexit announcement on June 24th, the value of bitcoin skyrocketed, gaining more than 9%, while all financial centers plunged for more than a week. This was probably the first time that the true strength of Bitcoin was shown to the world. In fact, BTC is an asset that does particularly well when there is turbulence in the world. We have seen this in 2020, where it rose by over 600% in just one year.

In 2017, Bitcoin topped out at around $19,000 and entered a long bear market of over 2 years. Those who accumulated during that time were brave enough to survive more than 700 days without seeing the asset climbing back to its all time high. However, in 2020, Bitcoin finally managed to break that level and skyrocketed. At the time of writing this book, one bitcoin is worth around $60,000.

Think about it, if you bought $10 worth of Bitcoin on February 9th, 2011, you would now have an equivalent of over $600,000. These kind of numbers really impress us.

Chapter 3 - The Idea behind Bitcoin

B itcoin's theoretical roots lie in the Austrian school of economics and its critique of the current monetary system and interventions by governments and other entities, which this school of thought says exacerbates business cycles and massive inflation.

One of the topics that the Austrian School of Economics, led by Eugen von Böhm-Bawerk, Ludwig von Mises and Friedrich A. Hayek, focused on is the business cycle. In fact, according to the Austrian theory, business cycles are the consequence of inevitable monetary interventions in the market, whereby an excessive expansion of bank credit leads to an increase in the stock of bank credit in a fractional reserve system, which in turn leads to artificially low interest rates.

In this situation, entrepreneurs, guided by distorted interest rate signals, embark on over-ambitious investment projects that do not match the preferences of consumers at that time for intertemporal consumption (that is, i.e. their short-term decisions and future consumption). Sooner or later, this generalized imbalance can no longer last and leads to a recession, during which companies must liquidate failed investment projects and restructure their production structures according to the intertemporal preferences of consumers. As a result, many economists in Austrian schools are calling for the abandonment of this process by abolishing the fractional reserve banking system and reverting to a currency based on the gold standard, which cannot be easily manipulated by authorities.

A related area in which Austrian economists have been very active is monetary theory. Friedrich A. Hayek is one of the best known names in this field. He wrote some very influential publications, such as Denationalization of Money (1976), in which he postulated that governments should not have a monopoly on issuing money. On the contrary, he suggests that private banks should be allowed to issue non-interest bearing certificates, based on their own trademarks. These certificates (i.e. currencies) should be open to competition and would be traded at varying exchange rates. Any currency that can guarantee stable purchasing power would eliminate other less stable currencies from the market. The result of this process of competition and profit maximization would be a highly efficient monetary system in which only stable currencies would coexist.

The following ideas are generally shared by Bitcoin supporters.

- They see Bitcoin as a good starting point to end the monopoly of central banks in issuing money.

- They strongly criticize the current fractional reserve banking system, which allows banks to extend their credit supply beyond their actual reserves and, at the same time, allows depositors to withdraw their funds to their checking accounts at any time.

Specificity of Bitcoin

We must distinguish between bitcoin, cryptocurrency and on the other hand Bitcoin, the payment system in this currency. In these two aspects, Bitcoin differs from pre-existing systems on some important points.

First of all, unlike other monetary currencies, Bitcoin is not the embodiment of the authority of any state, bank, or business. The value of bitcoin is determined in a fully floating fashion by the economic use that is made of it and by the foreign exchange market. The rules organizing the monetary issue are determined solely by the free computer code of the Bitcoin software.

Furthermore, as a payment system, Bitcoin is distinguished by the fact that its operation does not require the use of a centralized infrastructure keeping accounts of the amounts held in order to ensure transactions. The role of guarantee and verification exists, but is assigned approximately every ten minutes to a computer of the network chosen at random according to its power.

Bitcoin is based on a cryptographic protocol whose main purpose is, on the one hand, to resolve the so-called double payment problem, which had hitherto prevented the emergence of such a type of currency, and, on the other hand, to "prohibit" the falsification of stakeholder identifiers and the value of bitcoin stock in electronic wallets identified by a given address.

Monetary principles behind Bitcoin

From a monetary point of view, bitcoin is distinguished from other currencies by the major fact that the monetary aggregate is not designed to adapt to the production of wealth.

The total amount and the emission rate of the units are entered explicitly in the computer code of the software, according to a mathematical rule of the geometric series type. Bitcoins are issued slowly and steadily, decreasingly, reaching a maximum amount of 21 million around the year 2140.

All fiat currencies experience inflation, from low to high depending on the policies of their central bank. Conversely, bitcoin currency is likely to end up experiencing deflation, as the maximum amount of bitcoins that can be created is set in the software in advance at 21 million. In addition to this, bitcoins lost by users will never be replaced. This is why the Bitcoin project is considered by the community of its creators as an original experiment in economic terms, constituting a kind of test of the monetary theses of the Austrian school of economics. In fact, Friedrich Hayek, Nobel laureate in economics, in 1976 called for the reestablishment of monetary free will in his book "For a true competition of currencies". The success or failure of Bitcoin is difficult to predict, but it is impossible to say it has not done well so far.

Scalability of the protocol

On July 14th, 2010, shortly after the launch of the Bitcoin system, Satoshi Nakamoto created a limit of 1MB for each newly created block every ten minutes on the bitcoin blockchain.

At that time, transactions were free because few in number, and developers had a legitimate concern that attackers could "spam" the transaction network, arbitrarily creating huge blocks and permanently inflating the size of the blockchain. This limit was intended to prevent this kind of attack until a better solution could be put in place. Satoshi Nakamoto had proposed a solution that would involve increasing the block size to certain block heights, effectively increasing the limit to a predetermined rate similar to how new bitcoins are issued.

The scalability of the Bitcoin system has been a constant source of debate in the community since the introduction of this block size limit. This 1 MB limit, initially thought to limit the number of transactions per second to seven, posed no problem at a time when the actual number of transactions hardly exceeded 2.3 transactions per second (2010). So, seven transactions per second was three times the volume of bitcoin's busiest day at that time, leaving developers years to find a better solution. In addition to this, the protocol provided for the introduction of transaction fees over time, which would make this type of attack more costly and ineffective.

Saturation of transaction integration capacity

From 2014, the success of the Bitcoin system led to a continuous rise in the number of transactions which eventually hit the 1MB limit in 2016. A developer, Gavin Andresen, initially proposed 20MB blocks, but the increase was deemed too aggressive by the community. Another proposal, BIP10191, offered to increase the block size by 40% per year from 8MB which led to the creation of a new cryptocurrency, different from bitcoin, called Bitcoin XT92. Other proposals have been made like BIP10093 with a 2MB block which leads to the Bitcoin Classic cryptocurrency and more aggressive "emerging consensus" approaches that allow users to "vote" on the best block size at a time given through Bitcoin Unlimited.

Other members of the community preferred not to favor an increase in the block size, but to change the protocol itself so that more transactions are integrated in a block by reducing their size or increasing the creation frequency of new blocks.

When the number of transactions eventually reached the block size limit, the pool of pending transactions became full. The only way to get a given transaction into the blockchain faster for a user was to increase transaction fees, which reached nearly $5 at the end of 2016. This made Bitcoin uncompetitive against existing services like Western Union or Paypal on the strict basis of speed and cost.

The New York Agreement

The stalled debate on scalability weakened the Bitcoin Core system and led to the growing success of the vote in favor of the Bitcoin Unlimited movement, especially among miners, in large part due to frustration at the lack of upgrading solutions. The approach of the development team, called segwit (segregated witness), of not increasing the block size limit, but differently partitioning the digital signatures of transactions into "extension block", was not working to achieve sufficient consensus.

A compromise was found in an industry consensus in 2017 called Segwit2x97, which combined the segregated witness proposal with a block size increase to 2MB. This proposal was implemented on August 1st, 2017 for segregated witnesses and the block size increase came into effect in November 2017 at block 494,784. It was a major update to the Bitcoin system.

Nonetheless, the scalability debate was still heated and a breakaway group unilaterally increased the block size to 8MB while rejecting the Segwit proposal on August 1, 2017. This decision led to the emergence of a new cryptocurrency, called Bitcoin Cash.

Bitcoin XT (created in August 2015), Bitcoin Unlimited (created in January 2016), Bitcoin Classic (created in February 2016 before being discontinued in November 2017), Bitcoin Cash (created in August 2017) and Bitcoin Gold (created in October 2017) are alternative cryptocurrencies to Bitcoin (also called Bitcoin Core) that try to solve the problem of transaction fees.

Distribution of wealth

Bitcoins are concentrated in the hands of a few whales. The distribution of "wealth" is such that 2,100 addresses hold 40.2% of the total. However this kind of information is not very useful because some of these addresses are dead (keys lost when a unit of bitcoin was not worth 1 cent). Our opinion is that now that we are seeing institutions jumping on board, we will have much more concentration in terms of the number of bitcoins owned by whales. As the price rises, it will be more and more difficult for the average Joe to have ownership of one full bitcoin.

Chapter 4 - How Bitcoin Works

B itcoin does not have an independent existence of the Bitcoin payment system which allows transactions to be made from one account to another, thanks to software called wallets, and the authority being ensured by software from verification called miners. The data of all transactions constitute a public ledger under private law called "blockchain" because of its structure, and an agent uses bitcoins by recording their transactions in the Bitcoin system's blockchain.

The Bitcoin system is computer-based. In other words, the Bitcoin system resides on the Internet. Downloading and installing the appropriate software allows you to become a Bitcoin user by interacting with hardware of your choice, including a smartphone or computer. To pay or be paid in bitcoin, the user must connect to the system. This connection offers two functions: the creation of any number of accounts, and the ease of carrying out transactions consisting of the transfer of bitcoins from an own account to the account of a third party.

The essential function of the Bitcoin system lies in the transactions which are subjected to a validity check by the competent computers and are irrevocably entered in a public register. This public ledger or blockchain can be viewed anywhere by anyone, as long as they have an internet connection. During the consultation no alteration is possible.

Bitcoin transaction mechanism

A Bitcoin transaction requires two fundamental steps.

First, dedicated network nodes (the "miners") create a new block by grouping together recently completed transactions and adding a header to them containing the date and time, a checksum ("hash "), which will also serve as the unique identifier of the block, and the identifier of the previous block.

Secondly, after having checked the validity of all the transactions contained in this new block and their consistency with the transactions already recorded, each miner adds it to their local version of the register (or chain of blocks).

The public register is copied several times. The complete history of all transactions can then be read by viewing all nodes in the network that manage a copy of the blockchain. The copy can reveal possible differences between files, in the event of disagreement. In this case, any differences between these copies must be resolved by the software.

If you think about it, transactions consist of debiting certain accounts in order to credit others.

They are made up of inputs and outputs. Each output includes an amount and the public key of the credited address, or more generally a program (a script) making it possible to authorize or not the transfer of the amount of this output to another transaction. Each input designates an output from a previous transaction and has a program (script) that provides the data expected by the script appearing in that output. The sum of the values of the outputs must be less than or equal to the sum of the values of the inputs. The difference constitutes the miner's remuneration.

When creating a transaction, scripts for each entry are executed; first the script of the entry itself, then the script of the earlier exit that the entry refers to. The transaction is only committed if the result is "true" for all inputs.

These scripts are written in an internal language designed by Nakamoto. This language is intentionally minimalist and not

Turing-complete in order to prevent the system from being able to engage in infinite loops. The use of scripts should allow the software to easily adapt to future developments and allow support for advanced features such as transactions involving multiple signatures or smart contracts.

Transactions made by a node are broadcast to its neighbors. These validate the transactions they receive and gradually consolidate them into a local pool before passing them on to their own neighbors. The valid transactions are thus broadcast step by step to all the nodes of the network, after a new check during each step.

Before permanently registering a transaction in the blockchain, the network performs several times a set of checks, including in particular that the outputs referenced by the inputs do exist and have not yet been used, that the author of the transaction is indeed the owner of the address credited in these outputs, and that the sum of the amounts appearing in the outputs of the transaction is much less than or equal to the sum of the amounts of the outputs referenced by the inputs. It is a bit complicated, but if you read this last sentence a couple of times you will get a better grasp of what actually happens during a transaction.

The effect of entering a transaction in the blockchain is to prohibit any future reference to the outputs designated by the inputs of this transaction, and therefore to prevent a double expenditure of the amount of these outputs, which would amount to creating from scratch bitcoins in an unauthorized manner. The only allowed creation of bitcoin from scratch is through a special transaction called Coinbase (not the exchange) inserted at the start of each block in the chain to pay the miner who inserted the block.

A transaction is taken into account instantly by the network and confirmed for the first time after approximately 10 minutes. Each new confirmation reinforces the validity of the transaction in the transaction register.

Bitcoin addresses

Each user can have any number of addresses that can be created through the wallet. Each bitcoin address has a public key and a private key pair associated with it.

An address is equal to the 160-bit (20 bytes) cryptographic hash of its public key. A bitcoin address also has a prefix identifying the version number (0 by default) and a four-byte checksum. In all, a bitcoin address occupies 25 bytes.

An address is represented in ASCII format thanks to a dedicated encoding of 58 alphanumeric characters: upper and lower case numbers and letters, with the exception of the letters and numbers l, I, o and O, which Nakamoto excluded due to their resemblance in some typefaces.

Here is, as an example, the very first bitcoin address that received bitcoins.

1A1zP1eP5QGefi2DMPTfTL5SLmv7DivfNa1o6.

To use the sum contained in an output of an existing transaction crediting a bitcoin address, the user must make use in the input of a transaction of the private key corresponding to the address by signing the transaction. The network checks the validity of this signature using the public key associated with the credited address, using asymmetric cryptography techniques. The operation is repeated for each entry of the transaction.

Wallets

Each user's wallet contains their personal data, including the address, public key and private key of each of their accounts. It can also contain user-specific information built from the blockchain. For example the list of available transaction outputs or account balances.

The wallet software provides the functions of creating accounts, consulting accounts, constructing and sending transactions. There is a choice of wallet software for all varieties of devices including smartphones. They differ in the extent of their ancillary functions and in their user interface.

The information contained in a user's wallet is critical and must be strictly protected against any intrusion. If the private key of an account is lost, the user can no longer access the transactions that fund this account, nor create new transactions from it. His bitcoins are permanently lost and will stay forever in the database without being able to change address. In 2013, a user lost 7,500 bitcoins, at the time worth $7.5 million, by accidentally throwing away the hard drive that contained his private key.

The discovery of the private key of an account by another user allows this one to steal the identity of the legitimate account holder and to spend the bitcoins which would come to be there, which is equivalent to the theft of bitcoins.

The mining process

The mining operation consists of assembling transactions into "blocks", by adding a header indicating in particular the size of the block, the number of transactions recorded, the date and time, a checksum ("hash") prohibiting any modification of the block and also serving as a unique identifier for the block, as well as the identifier of the previous block.

Miners include in the blocks they constitute a particular transaction which credits them with a certain number of bitcoins created for this purpose, and incorporates specific transaction fees. However, this remuneration will only be effective if the block is definitively accepted in the blockchain by the other nodes. It is this creation of money that explains the use of the term "mining", by analogy with the exploitation of gold mines.

A block can contain any number of transactions, typically between 1000 and 2000, but the block size cannot exceed 1 megabyte (for the Bitcoin Core system).

Within a block, transactions are stored in the form of a Merkle tree. The checksum (or fingerprint) of the block is calculated by applying twice a SHA-256 hash to the sextuplet made up of the following components.

- The software version number;
- the footprint of the header of the previous block;
- the root of the block's transaction tree (which is itself an indirect fingerprint of all the block's transactions);
- the timestamp (time elapsed since January 1, 1970, in seconds);
- the "nonce".

The calculation of this footprint is made intentionally difficult by the requirement to be less than a certain value, which is materialized by a binary representation starting with a certain number of zeros. To this end, the fingerprint contains among its components, an arbitrary 32-bit number, called the "nonce".

Even if one knows the hashes corresponding to certain nonces, the hashing makes it impossible to determine the value of the hash for a new nonce without running the algorithm again. Therefore, we can only find the appropriate nonce for the bound requirement on the value of the fingerprint by making several tests.

For a given value of the nonce, the probability of calculating a footprint less than the difficulty is very low, so many attempts must be made before this is achieved. Between 2014 and 2016, the average number of nonces that each miner had to test between each creation of blocks increased from 1 billion to 200 billion. This calculation consists of performing the same calculation a very large number of times from different data, so it lends itself well to parallel calculation.

The difficulty is readjusted every 2016 blocks to take into account the real computing power of the network and allows on average to add a block every 10 minutes, which amounts to saying that the probable duration of calculation of a valid footprint is 10 minutes for the most powerful computer or group of computers on the network.

This system of proof of work and chaining of blocks by their footprint makes any alteration of the blockchain practically impossible (except in the case of a 51% attack). An attacker who wishes to modify a transaction in a given block would be forced to recalculate his checksum and that of all subsequent blocks. As the difficulty increases over time, as does the number of blocks after the modified transaction (its degree of confirmation), the time required to make such a modification increases very rapidly.

When a miner has built a valid block whose checksum satisfies the difficulty condition, it broadcasts it to neighboring nodes, who check its validity before reposting it in turn. The remuneration for mining work is made in bitcoin. The payout is known as the block reward. The current block reward is 6.25 bitcoins. This reward is halved for every 210,000 blocks.

The valid blocks are thus broadcast step by step to all the nodes of the network, not without having been checked beforehand, but without being able to be modified. From the nonce included in the header, it is quick and easy to check the validity of the block (a simplistic parallel can be made with a sudoku game: its resolution is difficult and requires time and human calculation but its verification is very easy once the solution is found).

The environment dilemma

Mining is an activity often criticized because of the supposed environmental imprint of its energy consumption. However, some observers weigh down the criticism by pointing out that the "classic" monetary network consumes much more energy, through millions of cash dispensers or the infrastructures necessary for the proper functioning of the classic monetary system, such as data centers. The majority of bitcoin miners use renewable energy because it is cheaper in regions of the world that favor mining (low temperature, presence of dams, geothermal energy, etc.).

Estimate of power consumption

The power consumption of Bitcoin mining is difficult to assess due to the decentralization of the activity. The figures most often cited by the press come from the "Digiconomist" site created by a Dutch financial analyst.

According to his estimate, which is based on the assumption of an economic balance between mining revenues and costs, the global electricity consumption caused by mining would be 71.1 TWh / year (1 terawatt-hour (TWh) = 1 billion kilowatt-hours (kWh)). This would totat to about 0.32% of global electricity consumption.

With only around 200,000 transactions per day in 2018, Bitcoin's electricity consumption would be around 1,000 kWh per transaction on July 1st, 2018. By comparison Visa consumed 0.19 TWh / year to manage 111 billion dollars. transactions in 2017 (around 300 million transactions per day), i.e. 0.001 7 kWh per transaction. Bitcoin would thus consume approximately 600,000 times more energy per transaction than Visa. Note, however, that mining consumption is independent of the number of transactions.

The estimates of the "Digiconomist" site are nevertheless contested and considered exaggerated. In fact, according to Marc Bevand, a computer security engineer, they overestimate the power consumption of Bitcoin miners by a factor of 1.5 to 2.8 (probably 2.2), which would reduce the total power consumption to 32.3 TWh / year, or 424 kWh per transaction (the equivalent of the consumption of a 1000 W radiator operating for almost 18 days).

These estimates are marred by uncertainties due to the assumptions they require, but it is possible to calculate a minimum power consumption of the Bitcoin network from verifiable data.

- The number of hashes per second: 37.1×1018 H / s on July 1st, 2018;
- the power and chopping capacity of the most efficient machine on the market (Bitmain's Antminer S9): 1323 W for 13.5×1012 H / s.

It is thus possible to affirm that the Bitcoin network had at least 2.8 million mining machines on July 1st, 2018 and that its electricity consumption was at least equal to 32.2 TWh / year. The number of entities securing the Bitcoin network is constantly increasing which increases the value of bitcoins.

According to a Bank of America report published in March 2021, the bitcoin network consumed 0.4% of global electricity at the end of 2020, or about as much as the Netherlands, and emits as many greenhouse gases as oil burned by American Airlines. In two years, these emissions have increased by 40 million tonnes, the equivalent of 8.3 million cars, to reach 60 million tonnes. Three quarters of the world's mining capacity is based in China; 27% of Chinese miners are in Sichuan, a province with strong low-carbon hydroelectric production, but 43% are in Xinjiang, where 80% of electricity comes from coal-fired power stations.

Why is power consumption so important?

The very high energy consumption of Bitcoin is linked to the new block mining system, which is supposed to protect the system from fraud in the absence of a central authority. Security is based on a mathematical problem the solution of which is difficult to find and the resolution of which is inherently expensive. To have a chance of adding the next block to the chain, miners must indeed invest heavily in server farms in order to have great computing power. These farms use a lot of electricity to power and cool the servers.

To be able to register a new block on the blockchain, miners must solve a mathematical problem submitted to everyone who competes, and it is the first who finds a solution that proceeds to the registration and earns a fee in bitcoins. Since the solution can only be found by trial and error, it is the miner who is able to make the maximum number of tries who has the most chance of winning. The difficulty of the problem is adjusted so that the computation time necessary for its resolution is of the order of 10 minutes.

The magnitude of the electricity consumption is linked to the intensity of the calculations and to the fact that these calculations are made simultaneously by a large number of miners. It is linked to the price of Bitcoin, because the higher it is, the more the remuneration increases and the more miners there are. This is reminiscent of Henry Ford's prediction at the start of the twentieth century: "An energy currency will replace gold and end wars".

According to Fabrice Flipo and Michel Berne, of the Institut Mines-Télécom, the generalization of crypto-currencies could lead to an energy consumption greater than eight times the electricity consumption of France, i.e. twice that of the United States, because their security and the confidence we have in them are based on a mathematical problem whose answer is difficult to find and whose resolution is in essence expensive.

The optimization of equipment and technical progress would make it possible to consume only 417 MW by 2021, which would nevertheless require nearly 5,500 kWh to produce a bitcoin, i.e.

half of the annual electricity consumption of an American household.

Thus, for researcher Nicolas Houy, of the Lyon/Saint-Étienne Analysis and Economic Theory Group, "a large amount of money could very well be managed by a small amount of miners".

Groups of miners

The difficulty of mining has led miners to group together in mining pools to combine their computing resources and build new blocks more quickly. The remuneration corresponding to the constitution of each block is then divided proportionally between the members, after deduction of fees, which makes it possible to smooth their income and makes them less uncertain. In 2016, around ten of these cooperatives supplied 95% of the blocks. They are largely found in China (which accounts for most of the hash energy on the bitcoin network), but also in the Czech Republic and Georgia.

Remuneration for mining activities has led to the development of ever more specialized technologies. The most efficient hardware uses integrated circuits that outperform general-purpose processors while using less power. As of 2015, a miner not using equipment specially designed for mining had a low probability of covering his electricity and equipment costs, even by joining a mining group.

Chapter 5 - The Blockchain

The blockchain of the Bitcoin system is comparable to a public ledger recording transactions. It exists in more than 10,000 copies managed in parallel by the nodes of the network, none playing a privileged role. Some copies of the register are stored in areas safe from any cataclysm, such as in a bunker under the mountains in Switzerland.

The operator of each node in the network can decide to install a "full node" which builds and maintains a local copy of the blockchain. On the contrary, the operator can choose to be satisfied with a lightweight node which will call on the neighboring full nodes to validate the transactions using the SPV (simple payment verification) protocol.

Since these decisions are completely decentralized, it is impossible to know the number of nodes of each type. The only type permanently identified by specialized sites such as blockchain.info or bitnodes is that of "listening nodes" which accept, at the time of measurement, transactions and blocks from other nodes. Their number hovers around 10,000.

Network nodes are likely to number in the tens of thousands. For full nodes, the number of which matches the number of copies in the blockchain, estimates range from 5,000 to 30,000, located in 85 countries on all continents.

This redundancy ensures continuity of service. Each computer can become disconnected or crash without jeopardizing the proper functioning of the entire system. When it becomes operational again, the blockchain construction protocol it hosts automatically reconstructs the missing portion by resorting to neighboring nodes.

As long as they have access to the Internet, a user will always find a node in the network to accept and relay a write-in, and then there will be a large number of miners and full nodes, located all over the world, to register that write-up and make it accessible in the blockchain, where it will always remain accessible from any point in the world with Internet access, without being able to be modified.

This same redundancy, together with the "precautionary principle" under which each node of the network checks the validity of the information it receives before using it, makes it impossible to propagate fraudulent activities. Errors and frauds are still possible on a particular computer, whether caused by the operator of the site or by a hacker who manipulates this site; it is even possible that they are spread locally by contagion or by connivance. On the other hand, it is virtually impossible for such issues to spread to a significant percentage of the copies of the blockchain, let alone the entire network.

The construction of the blockchain

By receiving a new block, each computer managing a complete node executes a protocol leading either to the rejection of the block if it has already been received or if it is invalid, or to its addition to the local blockchain after a final check of all the writings it contains, or when it is put on hold.

Each block contains the identifier of the block that precedes it in its miner's blockchain and, in the most common case, this predecessor is the terminal block of the local chain, to which the new block is added after a final verification of its validity. The transactions contained in this new block are then validated by the node, in particular the one which pays in bitcoins the miner who created this block. This is transmitted to neighboring nodes and, step by step, to the entire network. In the event of failure during the verification of the validity of the block, it is kept pending, and is incorporated into a secondary branch of the blockchain.

If the node receives a new block that contains a transaction already present in the local chain, that block is rejected. It is therefore the first valid block received that each node will register in its chain of blocks. Identical blocks built by other miners in the same 10 minute cycle will be rejected, so the miners race to see their blocks added to the chain and are paid accordingly.

Due to the delay required for the blocks to propagate through the network, two blocks created in the same cycle can arrive in a different order depending on the receiving nodes, which then build different versions of the register. In this case, we say that there is a fork. Most of the time, a fork is temporary, and the blockchain construction protocol corrects it in the next cycle.

The consensus mechanism

In order for all copies of the blockchain to be identical on all nodes, even though they are built independently, this protocol incorporates a so-called "consensus" mechanism, which is a central part of the system. The rule used by Bitcoin is to retain the chain whose construction of the blocks that make it up has required the most important work. To this end, the header of each block indicates the difficulty of the work that was done to build it. The fact that the checksum of the block respects the imposed constraints constitutes the "proof of work" guaranteeing that this work has been carried out.

If, after adding a block to a secondary chain, it appears that the secondary chain required more work than the main chain, that secondary chain should become the main branch. To do this, the program goes back to where it was detached from the main branch, revalidates the blocks and the transactions they contain one by one, and adds each block at the end of the new chain being processed.

This very complex process is the real heart of the system because it is the only way to change the blockchain and its results are irreversible. It also provides functions such as the resolution of bifurcation cases and the reconstruction of the chain in the event of a computer or network shutdown.

At the end of this second phase, each of the thousands of copies of the blockchain that exist on the complete nodes was extended by a block chosen by each node from among the proposals of the

Bitcoin

miners by applying the programmed consensus rule. If all full nodes implement the same write and block validation rules, this additional block is the same for all nodes, so that all copies of the blockchain remain the same. A few thousand new transactions are thus recorded definitively and become accessible on the thousands of corresponding sites.

The role of cryptography

Cryptography is used to authenticate actors, but digital data is not encrypted: cryptography is only used to ensure the signature.

Signature keys

To be valid, each transaction must be signed, in the cryptographic sense of the term, using asymmetric cryptography techniques. To this end, each bitcoin address also constitutes the cryptographic fingerprint of a public key. Any transaction indicates as input the reference of a previous transaction justifying the availability of funds subject to the transaction and as output one or more bitcoin addresses and the amounts that

65

must be allocated to them. A transaction always balances its inputs and outputs.

To transmit bitcoins, a user must cryptographically sign a transaction referring as input to one or more previous transactions whose output amount is sufficient to cover the transaction. The private key used to sign this transaction must match the public key that previously received bitcoins. Therefore, the user must store all his private keys in a confidential and secure manner. The corresponding file in the software, called wallet.dat, must be kept and saved by the user in a confidential manner.

Cryptography enables the authentication and non-repudiation described above, through transaction signing and one-way functions. At no time does the system ensure the confidentiality or encryption of data transmitted over the network. All transactions are therefore in the clear.

The signing of transactions is performed using elliptical curve cryptography, known as ECDSA. In this case, the curve used is secp256k1.

Transparency

Even if the software does not use any personal data of the user, anonymity is not guaranteed. In fact, the identity of a user can be determined if the IP address is traceable, or possibly as a result of a meticulous and complex statistical study of the transaction database, or when the regulations of a state or group of states take legal steps to end the anonymity of transactions on virtual currency platforms. However, it is possible to remain anonymous on the Bitcoin network with so-called "mixing" services and a good knowledge of AML, and KYC measures applied to exchange platforms.

The Bitcoin system does not encrypt any of the data it uses. Cryptography is only used to create tamper-proof signatures and implement one-way functions. Only the private key wallet is likely to be encrypted by the user, but this is optional.

Proof of work

Bitcoin uses the proof of work method, initially imagined to solve the spam problem and in particular implemented in the Hashcash system. The hash algorithms are SHA-256 and RIPEMD-160. A double hash in SHA-256 is used to obtain the hash of the blocks and therefore the proof of work, while a SHA-256 followed by a RIPEMD-160 is used to construct the bitcoin addresses.

Bitcoin

Chapter 6 - The specific features of Bitcoin

The Bitcoin system's unit of account is bitcoin. The symbols used to represent it are BTC and XBT. Bitcoin can also be subdivided into smaller units such as millibitcoin (mXBT), microbitcoin (µXBT) or even satoshi, which represents 10 nano bitcoins (10nXBT). Microbitcoin is sometimes referred to as a bit.

The Unicode consortium agreed in November 2015 to add bitcoin among its characters, assigning it the code 20BF.

Specificities of Bitcoin

As a virtual currency, bitcoin has three particularities.

- In terms of regulation, the lack of legal status and regulatory framework means that virtual currencies do not provide any guarantee of price or liquidity. The voluntary limitation of the number of units issued without indexation carries a risk of speculation leading to high volatility.

- In terms of transparency, encryption of the identities of beneficiaries and order givers leads to total anonymity of transactions. The transactions carried out are recorded in a public register, but this traceability is limited. In fact, it does not allow to know the principal and the beneficial owner, it is neither certain nor systematic, it cannot be exploited neither technically nor legally.

- In terms of extraterritoriality, the protagonists, the servers and the legal persons who exploit them may be located in countries and territories whose cooperation may be difficult to obtain.

Exchange terminals allow bitcoin virtual currency to be exchanged for legal tender, much like an ATM can withdraw cash from a bank. To do this, these terminals can take into account identification formalities based on biometric control: taking palm prints, scanning an identity document and comparing facial features with the photo that appears on the identity card.

Another particularity of Bitcoin is the irrevocability of an illicit transaction, which makes it extremely important to be sure to send the funds to a correct address.

Proof of ownership

The user who owns bitcoins can access them through a specific address and a password also known as a private key. Since knowledge of the private key is essential for signing transactions, bitcoins cannot be spent without resorting to it. The network checks the validity of the private key using the user's public key with asymmetric cryptography techniques. On the other hand, only knowledge of the public key of an address is necessary to make a deposit. You can imagine the public key to be your bank account number, while the private key is the password to access your home banking.

Transactions and fees

Bitcoins from different transactions cannot be combined. A user receiving several payments will keep as many different amounts (called input data) in their wallet, even if their software, to make them easier to read, displays the total amount. When the user wants to spend them, their software will calculate the best set of input data to transfer to minimize the size of the output data and thus limit transaction costs.

Example: a user receives 13 payments of 1 × 2.3 XBT, 5 × 1.0 XBT, 2 × 0.7 XBT, 1 × 0.5 XBT, 1 × 0.3 XBT, 2 × 0.2 XBT and 1 × 0.1 XBT. The software will tell them that they have 10.0 XBT.
(Case 1): If they want to spend 3.0 XBT, the best set of output data will be to combine the 2.3 XBT and 0.7 XBT received previously.
(Case 2): If they want to spend 3.05 XBT, the best output data set is to bundle the 2.3 XBT with the 0.7 XBT received previously and split the transaction from 0.1 XBT into one exit transaction of 0.05 XBT, the other transaction fraction of 0.05 XBT being kept in the wallet.

As you can see, this process is quite complicated and requires a few internal transactions. The beauty of the Bitcoin network is that the end user does not need to do anything. Once the transaction has been issued, everything is done automatically.

The payment of transaction fees is theoretically optional, but the miners determine the order of processing of the transactions to be integrated into the new blocks according to the transaction fees offered by the users. The more a user accepts to pay high transaction fees, the faster their transaction will be processed. In the event of charges of the same amount, priority is given to the oldest transactions. Transactions made without transaction fees are processed after all others; in practice, these transactions start to be processed on average from 120 minutes and up to a potentially infinite time.

The most competitive transaction fees, which provide almost immediate confirmation, between 0 and 35 minutes on average, are around 80 satoshis / byte (0,000,000 80 XBT / byte). Thus, in 2016, for a median transaction size of 265 bytes, this represents an approximate cost of 21,200 satoshis (or less than $0.11) regardless of the amount of bitcoins to be transferred.

To discourage the proliferation of low-value transactions, the software applies a mandatory transaction fee of 0.0001 XBT to any transaction for an amount less than 0.01 XBT.

The larger the assemblies of input data are to carry out a transaction, the longer it takes to encode and the more the costs increase, while still remaining a very low overall amount. The algorithm of the Bitcoin software is designed to avoid as much as possible the aggregation of input data of amount less than 0.01 XBT in order to limit mandatory transaction fees.

If the amount of bitcoins to be transferred is low or if the transaction is recent, only the payment of transaction fees will allow immediate processing of the transaction. In fact, each transaction is assigned an order of priority determined as a function of its amount, its age and its size, itself determined as a function of the number of input data grouped together. Specifically, the software calculates a quotient determined by the number of bitcoins to be transferred multiplied by the age of the transaction and divided by the size of the aggregated input data. Below a certain quotient, the transaction will only be processed immediately in return for the payment of transaction fees.

If the user chooses not to pay transaction fees, the quotient will increase over time until it exceeds a threshold value which will trigger the processing of the transaction; it will thus be processed free of charge but with delay.

The higher the number of bitcoins to be transferred, the higher the quotient and the faster the user will see their transaction processed or free of charge.

For the same amount of bitcoins to be transferred, transactions involving a small number of input data are processed faster than others. Bitcoin software generally calculates the optimal fees to pay for the transaction to be processed at the time of transfer. These fees vary depending on the number of transactions to be processed at the time of the transfer, but overall they are very negligible. The user decides on their own how much transaction fees they are willing to pay.

Special cases

If a user has registered in their wallet 3 XBTs from two transactions of 1 and 2 XBT and wishes to purchase a product or service costing 2,999 XBT free of charge, the Bitcoin software will have to combine the two transactions and split the transaction of 1 XBT into one line of 0.999 XBT and one of 0.001 XBT. But in this case, the 0.001 XBT line would have an automatic charge of 0.0001 XBT applied. The user could not then make their purchase which would cost them 2 XBT + 0.999 XBT + 0.0001 XBT when they have 3 XBT and wish to keep 0.001 XBT. In such a case, it would be better for them to send 3 XBT to the seller free of charge, although some sellers want the exact purchase amount sent to them.

The reddit site reports the case of a user who won a jackpot of XBT 1,280 on a gambling site where the amount of bets was XBT 0.02. To transfer the jackpot amount, the gaming site had to aggregate 64,000 transactions amounting to XBT 0.02 in input data, which represented a 51,203 byte transaction; the amount of fees required for immediate processing was 0.026 XBT, or approximately $15, which is more than the player's bet amount, $12, or than a fee usually paid for a normal transaction- Some miners may choose to process transactions by breaking the rules of the Bitcoin protocol. In this case, they include the transaction in a new block that they will manage to mine in a longer time as their computing power is low.

The creation of bitcoins

The creation of a new block is rewarded with bitcoins created for this purpose. The amount of this reward is halved every time 210,000 transaction blocks are added to the blockchain. This process is called the "halving" and it is one of the fundamental reasons that sustain the price increase of bitcoin. Here is how it works.

From the creation of the first block (genesis block) to the 209,999th block, created on November 28, 2012, each miner was rewarded with 50 newly created bitcoins for the creation of a new valid block. From block 210,000 to block 419,999, created on July 9th, 2016, the reward was 25 bitcoins for each newly created block. From block 420,000 to block 629,999, created on May 11th, 2020, the reward was 12.5 bitcoins for each newly created block. From block 630,000 to block 839,999, the reward is 6.25 bitcoins for each newly created block.

The next halving should take place around May 2024, when the reward will decrease to 3.125 bitcoins per block.

The reward system tends towards zero as the series of 210,000 blocks follow one another, so that a maximum of 20,999,999.9769 bitcoins will be created, probably around the year 2140. The gradual decrease in the amount of new bitcoins rewarding the creation of new blocks will be offset by the development of transaction fees.

In other words, the inventor of the Bitcoin system tried to define a monetary policy whereby the number of bitcoins cannot exceed 21 million units in total, with the rate of creation of new units tending towards zero. Such a monetary system is described as deflationary. As you might know, the Dollar-based

system is inflationary, as more units are printed to sustain the
growth of the economy.

Confidentiality

The Bitcoin system indicates on the public ledger the amount of
bitcoins associated with each address. All transactions recorded
on the blockchain are also public. The identity of the owners of
bitcoin addresses is not public but can be determined, for
example through exchange platforms that record the identity of
their users.

Exchange platforms generally pool their users' holdings on a
single address and reallocate a bitcoin credit line to each of their
users through their trading software. Users can thus exchange
their bitcoins for other cryptocurrencies or for currencies. The
platform secures its deposits by distributing them over several
addresses or by storing them to prevent any theft. When a user
transfers the deposits from the platform to another address, the
platform debits the credit line and transfers the amount to be
exchanged from one of his addresses to the address indicated by
the user.

79

Researchers at Stanford University and Concordia University have shown that, to prevent hacking, bitcoin exchange platforms can prove their creditworthiness without revealing their addresses using zero-knowledge protocols.

It is also possible to keep bitcoins in "cold storage" on a digital medium disconnected from the network, which has the effect of protecting them against theft. Between 2017 and 2018, a French start-up sold more than 1.5 million of these bitcoin safes in 165 countries Nowadays, Ledger and Trezor are the two main companies that sell hard wallets.

Researchers have argued that in the absence of specific protection measures, payments made using the Bitcoin protocol are no more private than payments by bank card.

Stock exchanges and financial instruments

Bitcoin, as a virtual currency, is quite unclassifiable. Thus, some asset management companies consider that virtual currency can neither be considered as a good investment, nor be compared to gold, due to the lack of price history.

For the ex-president of the SEC, Jay Clayton, the "Initial Coin Offerings" are less protected than the traditional securities, allowing more manipulation of markets and scams. For him, as for other investments, extreme caution as well as awareness of the risk of losing everything is required.

No ICOs have been registered with the US federal financial markets regulator and supervisor (known as the SEC), and the listing and trading of exchange traded products that hold cryptocurrency has not been approved by the SEC up to this point.

Market platforms

Fiduciary currencies (USD, EUR, CNY, etc.) or crypto-currencies (ETH, LTC, etc.) can be exchanged for bitcoins through various exchanges or specialized trading platforms active on the internet, by carrying out transactions transfers by bank transfer. Brokerage fees are generally very low and users must provide proof of their identity to access these platforms. As you might think, in this way the anonymity of Bitcoin disappears.

Escrow platforms connect buyers and sellers to exchange bitcoins for cash, money orders, or bank transfers.

One-way points of sale make it possible to pay in bitcoins, subject to the payment of a fee, by debiting the corresponding amount in dollars on bank cards or prepaid cards.

Finally, there are vending machines which charge a generally higher commission.

Since November 2016, the Swiss Federal Railways have been offering, in conjunction with the company SweePay, the purchase of bitcoins from their train ticket machines, thus creating the largest bitcoin distribution network in the world.

Bitcoin

Chapter 7 - Satoshi Nakamoto

As we have seen, the creation of the Bitcoin network is still a mystery. In this chapter we try to gather all the information there is regarding the identity of Satoshi Nakamoto. Please, keep in mind that his identity has never been revealed and that we can only make assumptions on who he actually is.

Satoshi Nakamoto is the pseudonym of the inventor of the cryptocurrency Bitcoin.

In November 2008, Satoshi Nakamoto published the Bitcoin protocol on The Cryptography Mailing list on the metzdowd.com website. In 2009 he distributed the first version of the client software and later contributed to the project anonymously together with other developers, to finally withdraw from the Bitcoin community in 2010. The last contact from Satoshi Nakamoto was in 2011, when he claimed to have moved on to other projects and left Bitcoin in good hands with Gavin Andresen.

The theories about Satoshi Nakamoto's true identity are numerous. Nobody knows if it is a "he", a "she" or if it is more than one person. In Japanese "satoshi" means "clear, quick and wise thought". "Naka" can mean "medium", "inside" or "relationship". "Moto" can mean "origin" or "foundation". But it is not certain whether these meanings are useful to trace back to the person or group of people who invented the Bitcoin system.

It was originally thought to be Michael Clear, a graduate in cryptography from Trinity College but he denied. Others suspected Vili Lehdonvirta, a former Finnish game developer (but also a sociologist and economist), but he too has denied any connection with Satoshi.

Adam Penenberg, a professor at New York University, claims that behind the mysterious character there are three people: Neal King, Vladimir Oksman, Charles Bry. Penenberg's thesis is based on a Google search of some particular phrases of the bitcoin protocol that lead back to a patent request for updating and distributing cryptographic keys. The patent was applied for by King, Oksman and Bry, who denied having anything to do with bitcoin.

Nick Szabo, a computer scientist and cryptographer, has long been suspected of being Satoshi along with collaborator Laszlo Hanyecz. Both have always firmly denied, but in the next pages we are going to tell you more about Szabo, as he is the one we believe to be Satoshi.

Others think it is Martii Malmi, a Finnish developer, who dealt with Bitcoin from the very beginning by also creating the user interface of the system. There are also rumors about the creator of MtGox, Jed McCaleb, an American lover of Japanese culture and resident in Japan. Other theories instead lead to Donal O'Mahony and Michael Peirce, who wrote a paper on digital payments in e-commerce platforms.

In 2017, after a tip from a SpaceX employee, the idea appeared on the web that Elon Musk was hiding behind the pseudonym, a theory later denied by the entrepreneur himself on his Twitter account.

Craig Steven Wright

In December 2015, according to two investigative articles published by Wired and Gizmodo, Craig Steven Wright, an Australian entrepreneur, would be the creator of Bitcoin. Within hours, searches were carried out in Wright's home and office by the Australian Federal Police, however unrelated to the incident.

On May 2nd, 2016, Craig Steven Wright publicly claimed to be Satoshi Nakamoto. Wright revealed his identity to the BBC, The Economist and GQ. In order to prove his claim, he signed a message with the private encryption key associated with the first Bitcoin transaction. However, the validation of this signature is disputed and even if its validity were demonstrated, many cryptographic experts do not consider it a definitive proof, as it refers to the second block and not to the first created.

On May 4th, 2016, Wright promised to publish further evidence to prove his identity. However, the next day, he deleted all posts on his blog and published a note titled "I'm sorry" in which he declared that he was ready to publish more evidence but did not have the courage to do so. He ended the note with a "goodbye". In the same year Wright filed a copyright request for the Bitcoin white paper, originally written by Satoshi Nakamoto. However, the copyright request was denied due to insufficient proof of ownership.

Nick Szabo

We admit it: our opinion is that Nick Szabo is Satoshi Nakamoto. We have no actual proof of his identity, but after having researched this subject quite extensively this is our opinion.

Nick Szabo is a computer scientist, lawyer, and cryptographer known for his research on digital contracts and digital currency. He graduated from the University of Washington in 1989 with a degree in computer science.The expression and concept of "smart contracts" were developed by Szabo with the aim of bringing what he calls "highly evolved" practices of contract law, from the conception to the application of the protocols of contract between strangers on the Internet. Smart contracts are a major feature of cryptocurrencies and the programming language E.

Szabo worked for David Chaum, the inventor of electronic money "E-Cash" as a consultant in the mid-90s. In 1998, Szabo designed a decentralized digital currency mechanism which he called "Bit gold". Bit gold, not having received enough support, was never implemented, but was referred to as a direct precursor to the Bitcoin architecture.

In the principle of Bit gold, participants devote the power of their computers to solving cryptographic puzzles. The solved puzzles are sent to a public registry insensitive to the problem of the Byzantine generals, and assigned to the public key of the participant who solved the puzzle. Each solution is then integrated into the input data of the next challenge, creating an increasingly long chain. Until the majority of participants agree to a solution for the current riddle, the work of solving the next riddle cannot begin. It is a proof-of-work-type consensus model. This also makes it possible to manage the issuance of new Bit gold tokens as well as a means of checking their timestamp.

The main problem with transactions in digital form is the so-called double-spending problem. Once the data has been created,  reproducing it is a simple matter of copying and pasting. Most digital currencies solve the problem by ceding some control to a central authority that keeps track of the balance of each account. This was considered unacceptable by Szabo. In an interview he stated the following. "I sought to imitate as closely as possible in cyberspace the security and trust characteristics of gold, and the main one is that it does not depend on any central authority".

In 2008, a mysterious figure writing under the pseudonym Satoshi Nakamoto published a proposal for Bitcoin. As you know Nakamoto's true identity has since remained a secret, leading to speculation about a long list of people suspected of being Nakamoto. Although Szabo has repeatedly denied it, some people (including us) have speculated that he was Nakamoto.

Research by financial author Dominic Frisby provides circumstantial evidence of this, but, as he admits, no formal evidence that Satoshi is indeed Szabo. In a July 2014 email from Frisby, Szabo said, "Thanks for letting me know this. I'm afraid you are wrong in exposing me as Satoshi, but I'm used to this".

Nathaniel Popper wrote in the New York Times that the most convincing evidence regarding the creation of Bitcoin pointed to an American man of Hungarian descent by the name of Nick Szabo. In 2008, prior to the publication of Bitcoin, Szabo wrote a comment on his blog about the intention to create a working version of his hypothetical currency. This blog post is exactly what makes us think he is the actual inventor of this amazing monetary network.

Bitcoin

Chapter 8 - The Byzantine Generals Problem

I n the previous chapters, we have mentioned the Byzantine generals problem a few times. In the next few pages we are going to dive deeper into this subject and understand why Bitcoin offers an amazing solution to this issue.

The problem of the Byzantine generals is a computer problem on how to reach consensus in situations where errors are possible. In particular, in distributed computer systems there may be imperfect information for the failure of a component, such as a server, and it can appear inconsistent, non-functional and functioning for fault detection systems, presenting different symptoms to different observers.

The problem

The problem of the Byzantine generals refers to a problem of agreement (described by Leslie Lamport, Robert Shostak and Marshall Pease in their 1982 article "The problem of the Byzantine generals") in which a group of generals commands part of the Byzantine army. Surrounded by a city, these generals want to formulate a plan to attack it. In its simplest form, generals should only decide whether to attack or retreat, and some generals prefer to attack, while others prefer to retreat. The important thing is that each general accepts a common decision, as a solitary attack by some generals would result in a defeat and would be worse than a coordinated attack or a coordinated withdrawal.

The problem is complicated by the presence of traitorous generals who not only vote for a suboptimal strategy, but can do so selectively. For example, if nine generals vote, four of whom support the attack while the other four are in favor of the withdrawal, the ninth general can send a vote of withdrawal to those generals in favor of the withdrawal and an attack vote to the others. Those who have received a vote of withdrawal from the ninth general will withdraw, while the rest will attack. The problem is further complicated by the fact that the generals are physically separated and must send their votes through messengers who may not report the votes or falsify them.

Byzantine fault tolerance can be achieved if loyal (non-defective) generals find majority agreement on their strategy. Note that there may be a default vote value for lost messages. For example, missing messages can be assigned the value <null>. In addition, if the agreement provides that the <null> votes are the majority, it is possible to use a pre-established strategy (for example, withdrawal).

The typical mapping of this story into computer systems is that computers are the generals and their connections to the digital communications system are the messengers. Although the problem is formulated in the analogy as a decision-making and security problem, in electronics it cannot be solved simply with cryptographic digital signatures, since errors such as incorrect voltages can be propagated through the encryption process. Therefore, a component may appear to be functional for one component and defective for another component, which prevents a consensus on whether the component is defective or not.

Examples of Byzantine errors

In a similar problem, bee swarms are used as an example. They have to find a new home, and the bees have to reach a consensus on which of the candidate homes they can reach. And then everyone has to fly there, with their queen. The bee approach works reliably, but when researchers find two houses, equally attractive by all bee criteria, a catastrophe occurs, the swarm breaks up and all the bees die.

First solutions

In 1982 Lamport, Shostak and Pease described several solutions. They began by pointing out that the problem of generals can be reduced to solve a "commander and lieutenant" problem in which loyal lieutenants must act in group and that their action must correspond to that the commander has ordered in case the commander is loyal.

One solution considers scenarios in which messages can be falsified, but which will be tolerant of Byzantine flaws as long as the number of traitorous generals does not equal or exceed one third of the generals. The inability to deal with a third or more of the traitors ultimately boils down to proving that the problem of one commander and two lieutenants cannot be solved if the commander is a traitor. To see this, suppose we have a treacherous commander A and two lieutenants, B and C. When A tells B to attack and C to retreat, and B and C exchange messages, relaying the message from A, neither B nor C can find out who the traitor is, since it is not necessarily A. In fact, another lieutenant could have falsified the message presumably from A.

It can be shown that if "n" is the number of generals in total, and "t" is the number of traitors in that n, there are solutions to the problem only when n>3t and the communication is synchronous.

A second solution requires unforced message signatures. For critical security systems, digital signatures (in modern computer systems, this can be achieved in practice using public key cryptography) can provide tolerance to Byzantine flaws in the presence of an arbitrary number of traitorous generals.

There is also a variation of the first two solutions that allow for behavior tolerant to Byzantine errors in some situations where not all generals can communicate directly with each other.

Around 1980, several system architectures that implemented Byzantine fault tolerance were designed. These include: Draper's FTMP, Honeywell13's 12 MMFC, and SRI.14's SIFT

Fault tolerance

In 1999, Miguel Castro and Barbara Liskov introduced the "BFT (Byzantine Fault Tolerance) algorithm. In a nutshell, Byzantine fault tolerance (BFT) is the property of a system that can resist the class of failures derived from the Byzantine generals Problem. This means that a BFT system is able to continue operating even if some nodes fail or act dishonestly.

There is more than one solution to the Byzantine generals problem and, consequently, more than one way to build a BFT system. Likewise, there are various different approaches for a blockchain that intends to achieve Byzantine fault tolerance. This brings us to so-called consensus algorithms.

Bitcoin and the BFT algorithm

An example of BFT in use is bitcoin, a peer-to-peer digital currency system. The bitcoin network works in parallel to generate a Hashcash-style work test chain. The proof-of-work chain is the key to overcoming Byzantine failures and obtaining a coherent global view of the state of the system.

We can define a consensus algorithm as the mechanism by which a blockchain network achieves consensus. The most common implementations are proof of work (PoW) and proof of stake (PoS). Let's take the case of Bitcoin as an example.

While the Bitcoin protocol establishes the primary rules of the system, the PoW consensus algorithm is what defines the way these rules are followed to reach consensus (for example, when verifying and validating transactions). Even though the concept of proof of work is older than cryptocurrencies, Satoshi Nakamoto developed a modified version by creating an algorithm that allowed the creation of Bitcoin as a BFT system.

It should be remembered that the PoW algorithm is not 100% Byzantine fault tolerant, but thanks to the expensive mining process and the underlying cryptographic techniques, PoW has proved to be one of the safest and most reliable implementations for blockchain networks. In this sense, the Proof of Work consensus algorithm, designed by Satoshi Nakamoto, is considered by many to be one of the most ingenious solutions to the Byzantine Generals Problem.

As we have seen, the Byzantine Generals Problem is an interesting dilemma that eventually gave rise to BFT systems, which are widely applied in different scenarios. In addition to the blockchain sector, some use cases for BFT systems include aviation, space industry and nuclear energy.

In the context of cryptocurrencies, having efficient network communication along with a valid consensus mechanism is vital for any blockchain ecosystem. Securing these systems is a constant effort, and existing consensus algorithms have not yet managed to overcome certain limitations (such as scalability). Despite this, PoW and PoS are very interesting approaches as BFT systems, and the potential applications are certainly inspiring widespread innovation.

Conclusion

Congratulations on making it to the end of this book, we hope you found some useful insights to take your cryptocurrency trading skills to the next level. As you should know by now, the world of Bitcoin is extremely complicated and there is a new "opportunity" every way you look. However, our experience tells us that only by taking things seriously and having a proper plan you can develop your investing skills to the point that you can actually accumulate wealth.

Our final advice is to stay away from the shining objects that the world of cryptocurrencies offers you every day. Simply dollar cost average into Bitcoin and study the world of cryptocurrencies in depth. After you have sufficient knowledge on what you are talking about, you can go ahead and invest into other cryptocurrencies. Analyze your results, improve your money management skills and become the master of your emotions.

As you can see, there are no shortcuts you can take. Easy money does not exist. What exists is the possibility to start from zero and work your way up to become a professional Bitcoin investor. The journey might be difficult, but it is certainly worth it.

To your success!

Charles Swing and *Masaru Nakamoto*

Charles Swing & Masaru Nakamoto

Bitcoin Trading

Learn the Indicators and Chart Patterns to Master the Cryptocurrency Market and Profit from the 2021 Crypto Bull Run – Discover how to Time the Market!

work can be in any fashion deemed liable for any hardship or damages that may befall them after undertaking information described herein.

Additionally, the information in the following pages is intended only for informational purposes and should thus be thought of as universal. As befitting its nature, it is presented without assurance regarding its prolonged validity or interim quality. Trademarks that are mentioned are done without written consent and can in no way be considered an endorsement from the trademark holder.

Charles Swing & Masaru Nakamoto

Table of Contents

Chapter 1 - The Most Important Cryptocurrency for Your Trading

Before diving deeper into the different cryptocurrencies we think you should trade and invest in, we feel it is important to have a discussion on the most important cryptocurrency you are going to use in your investing and trading career. No, we are not talking about Bitcoin. Stablecoins are going to be your main weapon, so study this chapter carefully.

What stablecoins are

Stablecoins are digital assets designed to simulate the value of fiat currencies such as the dollar or euro. They enable users to quickly transfer value around the world while maintaining price stability.

Cryptocurrencies like Bitcoin and Ethereum are famous for their volatility compared to fiat. This is a predictable feature, considering that blockchain technology is still very young and cryptocurrency markets are relatively small. The fact that the value of a cryptocurrency is not pegged to any asset is interesting from a free market perspective, but it can be tricky when it comes to usability.

As a medium of exchange, cryptocurrencies are excellent from a technological point of view. However, fluctuations in their value have made them high-risk investments, and not exactly ideal solutions for making payments. By the time a transaction is settled, the coins could be worth a lot more than when they were sent.

Stablecoins don't have this problem. These assets see negligible price movements and closely track the value of the underlying asset or fiat currency they simulate. For this reason, they are considered safe haven assets amid volatile markets. There are several ways a stablecoin can maintain its stability. In this chapter, we will discuss some of the mechanisms employed, their advantages, and their limitations.

How stablecoins work

There are several categories of stablecoins, each with a different method regarding anchoring its units. Here are the most common types of stablecoins.

Stablecoin backed by fiat

The most common type of stablecoin is directly backed by fiat money with a ratio of 1: 1. We call this category fiat collateralised stablecoins. A central issuer (or bank) holds a sum of fiat money in its reserves and issues a proportionate amount of tokens.

For example, the issuer could own a million dollars, and distribute a million tokens worth one dollar each. Users can freely trade these tokens as they would any other cryptocurrency, and at any time, they can redeem them for their USD equivalent.

It is clear that this type of stablecoin presents a high level of counterparty risk that cannot be mitigated: after all, the user must trust the issuer. There is no way to determine with certainty whether the issuer owns the funds in its reserves. At best, the issuing company can try to be as transparent as possible regarding audit posting, but the system is far from trustless.

Crypto-backed stablecoins

Crypto-backed stablecoins mirror their fiat-backed counterparts, with one central difference: cryptocurrencies are used as collateral. Furthermore, since cryptocurrencies are digital, smart contracts manage the issuance of units.

Crypto-backed stablecoins minimize the trust needed, but it should be emphasized that their monetary policy is determined through votes within the context of their governance systems. This means that you are not trusting a single broadcaster, but believe that all participants in the network will always act in the best interests of the users.

To obtain this type of stablecoin, users lock their cryptocurrencies into a contract, which issues the tokens accordingly. Then, to recover the collateral, they deposit the stablecoins in the same contract (along with any interest) and the redemption takes place automatically.

The specific mechanisms that regulate the anchoring vary according to the designs of each system. In general, a mix of game theory and on-chain algorithms incentivize participants to keep the price stable.

Algorithmic stablecoins

Algorithmic stablecoins are not backed by fiat or cryptocurrencies. Instead, their anchoring is carried out entirely through algorithms and smart contracts that manage the supply of the issued tokens. Functionally, their monetary policy mirrors that used by central banks to manage national currencies.

Essentially, an algorithmic stablecoin system will reduce the supply of the token if the price falls below the fiat currency it is tracking. If the price surpasses the value of the fiat currency, new tokens are put into circulation to reduce the value of the stablecoin.

You may hear the term uncollateralized stablecoins associated with this category, but it is incorrect on a technical level, as they are effectively collateralized - albeit not in the same way as the previous two types. In the event of a black swan event, algorithmic stablecoins may have some kind of collateral pool to handle particularly volatile market movements.

One of the most famous algorithmic stablecoins is Ampleforth.

Use cases for stablecoins

Collateralized stablecoins are by far the most common on the market. Examples of these coins include USD Tether (USDT), True USD (TUSD), Paxos Standard (PAX), USD Coin (USDC), and Binance USD (BUSD). However, there are also stablecoins of the other two mentioned categories currently available on the market. Bitshares USD and DAI are crypto-collateralized currencies, while Carbon and Basis are examples of algorithmic versions.

This list is certainly not exhaustive. The market for stable digital currencies is large, as evidenced by the proliferation of hundreds of stablecoin projects.

Pros and cons of stablecoins

The main advantage of stablecoins is their potential to provide a medium of exchange that complements cryptocurrencies. Due to the high levels of volatility, cryptocurrencies have not yet managed to achieve widespread use in everyday applications such as payment processing. By offering higher levels of predictability and stability, these stabilized currencies solve this problem.

By acting as a safeguard against volatility, stablecoins may also be able to play an important role in integrating cryptocurrencies with traditional financial markets. At present, these two markets exist as separate ecosystems with very few interactions. With a more stable form of digital currency available, cryptocurrency is likely to see greater use in the loan and credit markets, hitherto dominated exclusively by government fiat currencies.

In addition to their usefulness in financial transactions, stablecoins can be used by traders and investors as a hedge for their portfolios. Allocating a certain percentage of a portfolio to stabilized currencies is an effective method of reducing overall risk. At the same time, maintaining a store of value that can be used to buy other cryptocurrencies when prices fall can be a valid strategy. Additionally, these coins can be used to "lock in" the gains made when prices rise, without having to withdraw.

Despite their potential to support the widespread adoption of cryptocurrencies, stablecoins still have some limitations. The fiat collateralized variants are less decentralized than ordinary cryptocurrencies, as a central entity is required to hold the supporting assets. As for crypto-collateralized and uncollateralized currencies, users need to trust the general community (and source code) to ensure the longevity of the systems. We are talking about new technologies, so they will take some time to mature.

In the next chapter we are going to talk about Tether, the only stablecoin we advise you to use on a regular basis.

Chapter 2 - Tether (USDT)

Tether is a key component of the cryptocurrency ecosystem. As of April 2021, Tether is the fifth largest cryptocurrency with a market cap of nearly $50 billion, behind only Bitcoin, Ethereum, BNB and XRP. Furthermore, it often records the highest trading volume in the industry, surpassing even Bitcoin.

But what exactly is Tether, and how can it help your trading?

What Tether is

Tether (USDT) is the world's first stablecoin (a cryptocurrency that simulates the value of a fiat currency). It was originally launched in 2014 under the name Realcoin by Bitcoin investor Brock Pierce, entrepreneur Reeve Collins, and software developer Craig Sellers.

USDT was initially issued on the Bitcoin protocol through Omni Layer, but has since migrated to other blockchains as well. In fact, most of its offering is on Ethereum as an ERC-20 token. Additionally, it is issued on several other blockchains, including TRON, EOS, Algorand, Solana, and OMG Network.

Tether has gone through a fair amount of success and controversy - like many of the major cryptocurrencies.

Especially in its early days, the USDT price was quite volatile, even reaching $ 1.2 at one point. However, since the beginning of 2019 the coin has experienced much lower volatility. This is likely due to the steady growth of its trading volume and the overall progress of the crypto markets.

How Tether (USDT) works

The usefulness of stablecoins lies in their relative stability, in contrast to more traditional crypto assets. As a stablecoin, Tether's appeal lies in its tethering, or anchor, to a fiat currency. Originally, USDT was pegged exactly to USD, with 1 USD held for every USDT in circulation.

As the original Tether white paper explains:
Each outstanding unit of Tether issued is backed at a 1: 1 ratio (i.e., one USDT Tether is one US dollar) by the corresponding unit of fiat currency in the reserves of Hong Kong based company Tether Limited.

Although the original 1:1 asset for Tether was USD, reserves have transformed to include collateral with other cash equivalents, assets and credits.

The importance of Tether

Tether bridges the gap between crypto and fiat currencies. It offers investors an easy way to get a 1:1 trade for the USD, without the inherent volatility of other cryptocurrencies.

Thanks to this stability, investors can hold a digital asset similar to a fiat currency but with the ability to exchange it for other currencies in the crypto markets. The main features mentioned below make Tether a popular currency - albeit not immune to risk.

- 1: 1 ratio (USD to USDT)
- Stability (if the dollar can be considered stable)
- Available on different blockchains
- Different use cases compared to traditional cryptocurrencies

Quick access to market stability

If the price of Bitcoin or other crypto assets is falling fast, you can quickly trade it for USDT instead of trying to withdraw.

Easy transfer of funds between exchanges

With Tether, you can move your funds between exchanges very quickly. This can also be useful for arbitrage with other currencies.

Trading on crypto-only exchanges

Some exchanges do not offer fiat deposits and withdrawals, but allow USDT trading. By getting Tether first, you can trade on these exchanges without worrying about market volatility or allocating your main trading funds to BTC (or other crypto).

Forex style trading

Since USDT is pegged to the dollar, you can engage in Forex-style trading by trading local (non-US) currencies for USDT when their value is high against the USD. After that, you can withdraw in local currencies when their price drops or exchange it for other assets.

Storing Tether

In addition to Binance and other crypto exchanges, you can store your USDT in various crypto wallets. These include web and mobile wallets (such as Trust Wallet), cold wallets or hardware wallets (such as Ledger) through third-party software wallets.

Since USDT is issued on a number of different blockchains, you will need to make sure that you are transferring to and from the same network.

So, be careful. If you use the wrong network you could lose your funds. For example, if you try to send USDT Omni to a USDT ERC-20 address, your transfer will most likely be lost.

Remember that, as of April 2021, USDT ERC-20 is the only type supported by Ledger. This means that USDTs on the Bitcoin (Omni Layer) blockchain cannot be transferred to Ledger hardware wallets.

Other cryptocurrencies from Tether

In addition to USDT, Tether also offers other stablecoins like the following ones:

- EURT: a Tether currency pegged to the Euro
- CNHT: a Tether coin pegged to the Chinese yuan
- XAUT: a Tether coin anchored to physical gold

Chapter 3 - Basic Chart Patterns

There are many different ways to analyze the financial markets using technical analysis (TA). Some traders use indicators and oscillators, while others base their analysis on price movement only.

Candlestick charts present a historical overview of prices over time. The idea is that by studying past movements in the price of an asset, recurring patterns could emerge. Candlestick patterns can tell a useful story about the asset represented, and many traders seek to take advantage of it in the equity, forex and cryptocurrency markets.

Some of the more common examples of these patterns are collectively referred to as classic graphic patterns. These are some of the most popular patterns, and many traders consider them reliable trading indicators. Why? Isn't it true that trading and investing means finding an advantage in something that others have ignored? Yes, but it's also about mass psychology. Since technical patterns are not bound by any scientific principle or physical law, their effectiveness largely depends on the number of market participants who pay attention to them.

Flags

A flag is an area of consolidation that goes against the direction of the longer-term trend and occurs after a strong price movement. It looks like a flag on a flagpole, where the flagpole is the impulse movement and the flag is the consolidation area.

Flags can be used to identify the potential continuation of the trend. The volume that accompanies the pattern is also important. Ideally, the impulse movement should occur with a high volume, while the consolidation phase should have a smaller and decreasing volume.

Bullish flag

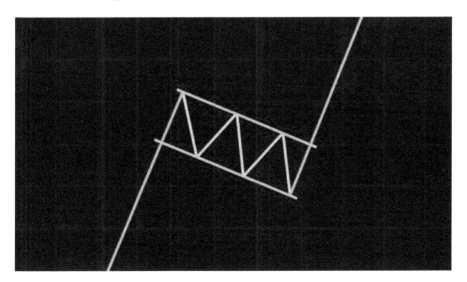

The bullish flag occurs in an uptrend, follows a strong upward movement and is usually followed by a further upward continuation.

Bearish flag

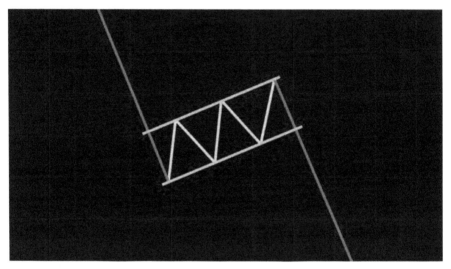

The bearish flag occurs in a bearish trend, follows a strong downward movement and is usually followed by a further downward continuation.

Pennant

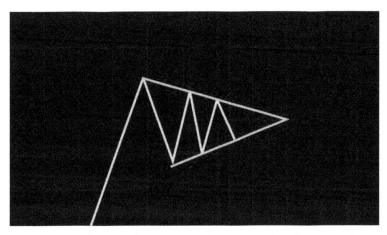

Pennants are basically a variation of flags where the consolidation area has converging trend lines, more like a triangle. The pennant is a neutral formation: its interpretation strongly depends on the context of the pattern and the market trend.

Triangles

A triangle is a chart pattern characterized by a converging price range, typically followed by the continuation of the trend. The triangle itself shows a pause in the underlying trend, but it could indicate a reversal or continuation.

Ascending triangle

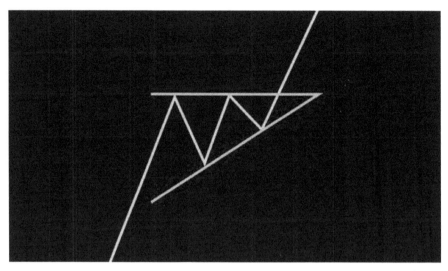

The ascending triangle forms with a horizontal resistance area and an ascending trend line marked by a series of rising lows. Essentially, whenever the price hits a horizontal resistance, buyers move to higher prices, creating rising lows. As tension develops in the resistance area, if the price manages to break the resistance, it tends to form a rapid movement with high volume. For this reason, the ascending triangle is considered a bullish pattern.

Descending triangle

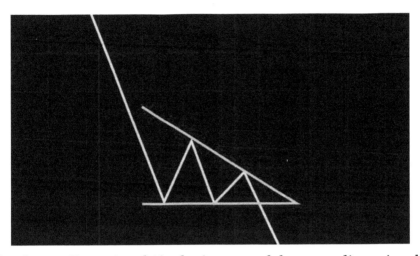

The descending triangle is the inverse of the ascending triangle. It forms with a horizontal support area and a descending trendline marked by a series of decreasing highs. As with the ascending triangle, each time the price bounces off the horizontal support, sellers move to lower prices, creating decreasing highs. Typically, if the price breaks the horizontal support area, a rapid downward movement with high volume follows. This makes it a bearish pattern.

Symmetrical triangle

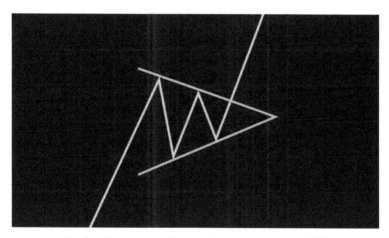

The symmetrical triangle is drawn by an upper falling trend line and a lower rising trend line, both with an approximately equal slope. The symmetrical triangle is neither a bullish nor a bearish pattern, as its interpretation is highly dependent on the context (i.e., the underlying trend). By itself, it is considered a neutral pattern, which simply represents a period of consolidation.

Wedges

A wedge is drawn from converging trend lines, indicating a contraction in price movements. Trend lines, in this case, show that the highs and lows are rising or falling at different rates.

It could mean that a trend reversal is on the way, as the underlying trend is weakening. A wedge pattern can be accompanied by decreasing volume, another indication that the trend is losing momentum.

Ascending wedge

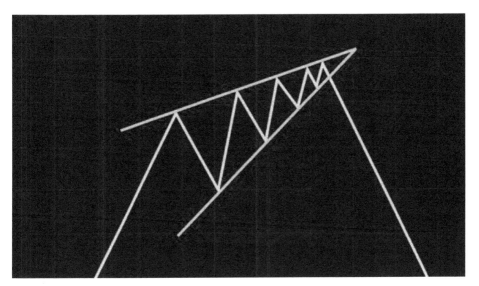

The ascending wedge is a bearish reversal pattern. It suggests that as the price contracts, the uptrend is weakening more and more, and could break the lower trendline.

Descending wedge

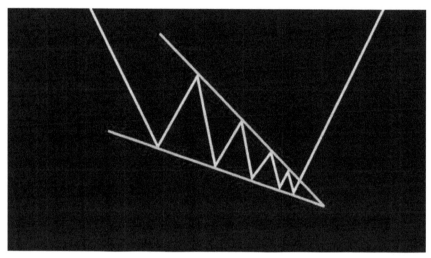

The descending wedge is a bullish reversal pattern. It indicates that the volume is increasing as the price falls and the trend lines get closer. A descending wedge often leads to an upward break with an impulse motion.

Double top and double bottom

Double tops and double bottoms are patterns that occur when the market moves creating an "M" or "W" shape. It is important to note that these patterns may be valid even if the relevant price points are not exactly the same but close to each other.

Generally, the two maximum or minimum points should be accompanied by higher volume than the rest of the pattern.

Double top

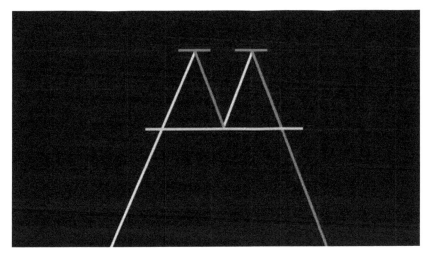

The double top is a bearish reversal pattern, where the price hits a top twice and fails to break it with the second attempt. At the same time, the pullback between the two highs should be moderate. The pattern is confirmed when the price breaks the lows of the pullback between the two highs.

Double bottom

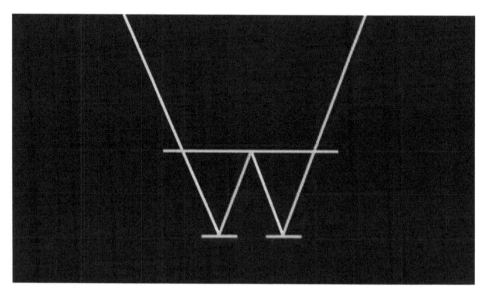

The double bottom is a bullish reversal pattern where the price holds a low twice and eventually continues with a higher high. As with the double top, the bounce between the two lows should be moderate. The pattern is confirmed when the price reaches a higher high than the high of the rebound between the two lows.

Head and shoulders

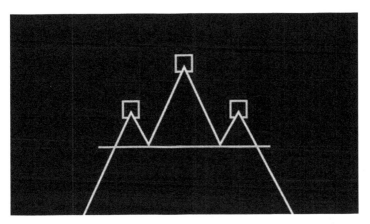

The head and shoulders is a bearish reversal pattern with a neckline and three peaks. The two side peaks should approximately reach the same price level, while the middle peak should be higher than the other two. The pattern is confirmed when the price breaks the neckline support.

Reverse head and shoulders

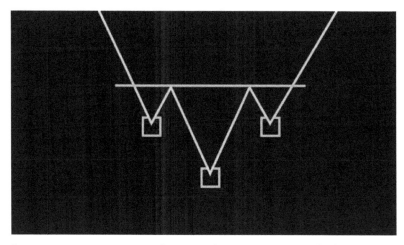

As the name suggests, this is the opposite of the head and shoulders - hence, it indicates a bullish reversal. A reverse head and shoulders forms when the price reaches a lower low during a bearish trend, then rebounds and finds support at about the same level as the first low. The pattern is confirmed when the price breaks the resistance of the neckline and continues upwards.

Classic chart patterns are among the best known TA patterns. However, as with any market analysis method, they should not be considered precise analysis tools. What works well in one market environment may not work in another. Therefore it is always advisable to seek confirmation, and at the same time apply adequate risk management as described in previous chapters.

Chapter 4 - Essential TA Indicators

Traders use technical indicators to gain additional insight into an asset's price movement. These indicators make it easier to identify buy or sell patterns and signals in the current market environment. There are many types of indicators, and they are used extensively by day traders, swing traders and sometimes even long-term investors. Some professional analysts and advanced traders even create their own indicators. In this chapter, we will briefly describe some of the most popular technical analysis indicators that can make a difference in any trader's arsenal.

Relative Strength Index (RSI)

The RSI is a momentum indicator that shows whether an asset is overbought or oversold by measuring the magnitude of recent price changes (the standard setting covers the previous 14 periods - so 14 days, 14 hours, etc.). The data is then represented as an oscillator which can have a value between 0 and 100.

Since the RSI is a frequency indicator, it shows the rate (or frequency) at which the price is changing. This means that if the momentum is increasing while the price is going up, the bullish trend is strong, and more and more buyers are coming. Conversely, if the momentum is decreasing while the price is rising, it could indicate that sellers will soon be able to take control of the market.

A traditional interpretation of the RSI notes that when it is above 70, the asset is overbought, and when it is below 30, it is oversold. As a result, extreme values could indicate a trend reversal or an upcoming pullback. However, it is best not to think of these values as direct buy or sell signals. As with many other technical analysis techniques, the RSI could provide false or deceptive signals, so it is always useful to consider other factors before opening a position.

Moving Average (MA)

A moving average smooths out price movements by filtering out noise and highlighting the direction of the trend. Being based on past price data, it is a lagging indicator.
The two most commonly used moving averages are the simple moving average (SMA or MA), and the exponential moving

average (EMA). The SMA is plotted by considering prices over a defined period and producing an average. For example, the 10-day SMA is plotted by calculating the average price over the last 10 days. The EMA, on the other hand, is calculated so that it gives more weight to recent prices. This method makes it more responsive to the most recent price movements.

As already mentioned, the moving average is a lagging indicator. The longer the period, the greater the data delay. For this reason, the 200-day SMA will react slower to recent moves than the 50-day SMA.

Traders often use the relationship between price and specific moving averages to identify the current market trend. For example, if the price remains above the 200-day SMA for an extended period of time, many traders may consider the asset to be in a bull market.

Traders can also use moving average crossovers as buy or sell signals. For example, if the 100-day SMA crosses below the 200-day SMA, it can be considered a sell signal. But what exactly does this intersection mean? It indicates that the average price over the last 100 days is now lower than the average price over the last 200 days. The reasoning behind this sell signal is that short-term price movements are no longer following the uptrend, so the trend may be nearing a reversal.

Moving average of convergence / divergence (MACD)

MACD is used to determine the momentum of an asset by showing the relationship between two moving averages. It consists of two lines - the MACD line and the signal line. The MACD line is calculated by subtracting the 26 EMA from the 12 EMA. This is then plotted on the 9 EMA of the MACD line. This is also called the signal line. Many charting tools integrate a histogram as well, representing the distance between the MACD line and the signal line.

By observing the divergences between the MACD and the price, traders could better understand the strength of the current trend. For example, if the price is marking a higher high while the MACD is at a lower high, the market may be close to a reversal. What is the MACD telling us in this case? That the price is rising while the momentum is decreasing, so there is a greater likelihood of a pullback or reversal.

Traders can also use the indicator to look for crosses between the MACD line and its signal line. For example, if the MACD line crosses above the signal line, this could suggest a buy signal. Conversely, if the MACD line crosses below the signal line, it could indicate a sell signal.

MACD is often used in conjunction with RSI, as they both measure momentum through different factors. The hypothesis is that together they can provide a more complete technical view of the market.

Stochastic RSI (StochRSI)

The Stochastic RSI is a frequency oscillator used to determine whether an asset is overbought or oversold. As the name suggests, it is a derivative of the RSI, generated from RSI values instead of price data. It is created by applying the Stochastic Oscillator formula to the ordinary values of the RSI. Typically, the Stochastic RSI values are between 0 and 1 (or between 0 and 100).

Due to its increased speed and sensitivity, the StochRSI can generate many trading signals which can prove difficult to interpret. Typically, it tends to be more useful as it approaches the upper or lower extremes of its range.

A StochRSI above 0.8 is generally considered overbought, while a StochRSI below 0.2 can be considered oversold. A value of 0 means that the RSI is at its lowest value in the measured period (the standard setting is generally 14). Conversely, a value of 1 indicates that the RSI is at its highest value over the measured period.

Similar to how the RSI should be used, an overbought or oversold value of the StochRSI does not mean that the price will reverse for sure. In the case of the StochRSI, it simply indicates that the RSI (from which the StochRSI is derived) is close to the extremes of its recent values. It is also important to keep in mind that the StochRSI is more sensitive than the RSI indicator, so it tends to generate more false or deceptive signals.

Bollinger Bands (BB)

Bollinger Bands measure market volatility, as well as overbought and oversold conditions. They consist of three lines - a simple moving average (the middle band), an upper and lower band. The settings may vary, but typically the upper and lower bands are two standard deviations away from the middle band. As volatility increases or decreases, the distance between the bands also increases and decreases.

Generally, the closer the price is to the upper band, the closer the analyzed asset could be to overbought conditions. Conversely, the closer the price is to the lower band, the closer it could be to oversold conditions. In most cases, the price will stay within the bands, but on rare occasions it may cross above or below them. While this event may not be a trading signal on its own, it can be an indication of extreme market conditions.

Another important BB concept is called squeeze. It refers to a period of low volatility, in which the three bands come close to each other. This could be used as an indication of potential future volatility. Conversely, if the bands are very far apart, a period of reduced volatility may follow.

Even if the indicators show data, it is important to consider that the interpretation of such data is very subjective. For this reason, it's always helpful to take a step back and consider if there are any personal biases that are affecting your decision-making process. What could be a direct buy or sell signal for one trader could be just noise for another.

As with most market analysis techniques, indicators work best when used in combination with one another, or with other methods, such as fundamental analysis.

In the next few chapters we are going to dive deeper into the different indicators we have mentioned up to this point. Please, take your time to study them in depth, as they are the foundation for a successful trading strategy.

Chapter 5 - Relative Strength Index (RSI)

The Relative Strength Index (RSI) is a TA indicator developed in the late 70s as a tool used by stock market participants to examine the performance of certain shares over a certain period of time. It is a market impulse oscillator that measures the magnitude and speed of price movements. The RSI can be a very useful tool depending on your approach to trading and is widely used by various traders and analysts.

In 1978, a mechanical engineer named J. Welles Wilder focused his analytical knowledge on technical trading. In the 60s he began his career in the real estate sector. In 1972, after selling his stake in the company, he used his $100,000 earnings to trade in the stock market. During these years he had been constantly looking for reliable tools to identify profitable trends. In 1978, Wilder compiled his research and experience in mathematical formulas and indicators for traders. The Relative Strength Index is one of these indicators.

How does the RSI indicator work?

The RSI measures changes in the price of an asset over 14 periods (14 days for daily charts, 14 hours for hourly charts and so on). The formula divides the average price increase by the average loss, so it places this force on a scale from 0 to 100.

As already mentioned, the RSI is an impulse indicator, a type of tool for technical analysis that measures the speed at which the price is changing. When the impulse grows, it indicates that the asset is actively bought in the market. If the impulse decreases, it signals that the interest of traders in the asset is decreasing.

The RSI is also an oscillator that allows traders to more easily identify overbought or oversold market conditions. Evaluate the price of the asset on a scale from 0 to 100, considering the 14 periods. A RSI score of 30 or less suggests that the asset is probably close to support (oversold). A score above 70 suggests that the price is close to resistance (overbought) for that period of time and is likely to fall back.

Although the standard settings for the RSI use 14 periods, traders can change it to increase sensitivity (fewer periods) or decrease sensitivity (more periods). Hence, a 7-day RSI is more sensitive to price movements than one considering 21 days.

Furthermore, short-term setups could adjust the RSI indicator to consider 20 and 80 as oversold and overbought levels (instead of 30 and 70), in order to reduce erroneous signals.

RSI divergences

In addition to the RSI scores of 30 and 70 - which can suggest potential oversold and overbought market conditions - traders can use the RSI to try to predict trend reversals or to find support and resistance levels through the use of so-called bullish and bearish divergences.

A bullish divergence is a condition where an asset's price and RSI scores move in opposite directions. Hence, the RSI score increases creating rising lows while the price decreases, creating decreasing lows. This situation is called a "bullish" divergence and indicates that the momentum is getting stronger despite the drop in the price.

On the contrary, bearish divergences may indicate that despite the price increase, the market is losing momentum. Therefore, the RSI score decreases creating decreasing highs while the asset price increases creating increasing highs.

However, remember that RSI divergences are not very reliable during strong market trends. This means that a strong downtrend could present several upward divergences before reaching actual support. For this reason, RSI divergences are more suitable for less volatile markets.

Using the RSI

There are several important factors to consider when using the Relative Strength Index, such as the settings, the score (30 and 70), and the up / down divergences. Also, remember that no technical indicator is 100% efficient - especially when used alone. Therefore, traders should consider using the RSI indicator together with other tools to be able to reduce the amount of incorrect signals.

Chapter 6 - Moving Averages

There are different types of moving averages that can be used by traders not only for day trading and swing trading but for long-term investing strategies as well. Despite the various types, MAs are typically divided into two separate categories: simple moving averages (SMA) and exponential moving averages (EMA). Depending on the market and the desired outcome, traders can choose which indicator is best suited for their strategy.

Simple Moving Average

The simple moving average takes data from a given period and produces the average price of the asset. The difference between a simple moving average and a base average of past prices is the fact that with the simple moving average, as soon as a new data set is entered, the old one is ignored. So, if the simple moving average calculates the average based on 10-day data, the entire data set is constantly updated to include the last 10 days.

It is important to note that all data entered in a simple moving average have equal weight, regardless of how recent they are.

Some traders believe that the most recent data is more important and that the equal weight of the SMA is detrimental to technical analysis. The exponential moving average was created to address this issue.

Exponential Moving Average

Exponential moving averages are similar to simple moving averages in that they provide technical analysis based on past price movements. However, the equation is more complicated because an exponential moving average assigns more weight and value to the most recent price inputs. While both averages are valid and widely used , the exponential moving average is more sensitive to sudden price reversals and fluctuations.

As exponential moving averages are more likely to predict reversals faster than simple moving averages, they are often favored by traders who use short-term strategies. It is important for a trader or investor to choose the type of moving average that best suits their goals and strategies, adjusting the settings accordingly.

Using moving averages in the best way

Moving averages use past prices instead of current prices, so they have a certain lag period. The more expansive the data set, the greater the delay. For example, a moving average that looks at the last 100 days will react to new information much more slowly than a moving average that looks at only the last 10 days. This is due to the simple fact that a new input into a larger data set will have a smaller effect on the overall number.

Either case can be beneficial depending on the trading strategy. Larger data sets favor long-term investors, as they are less likely to be heavily modified by one or two large fluctuations. Short-term traders prefer a smaller data set which allows for more reactionary trading.

Within the traditional markets, the 50, 100 and 200 day moving averages are the most used. The 50-day and 200-day moving averages are closely followed by stock traders and any move above or below these lines is usually considered an important trading signal, especially when followed by crossovers. The same is true for cryptocurrency trading, although due to its volatile 24/7 markets, moving average settings and trading strategy can vary depending on each trader's profile.

Crossover signals

Of course, a rising moving average suggests an uptrend and a decreasing moving average indicates a downtrend. However, a moving average alone is not a really reliable and strong indicator. As a result, moving averages are used in combination to detect bullish and bearish crossover signals.

A crossover signal is created when two different moving averages cross in a chart. A bullish crossover (also called golden cross) occurs when the short-term moving average crosses the long-term one upwards, suggesting the beginning of an upward trend. Conversely, a bearish (or death cross) crossover occurs when a short-term MA crosses a long-term downward trend, indicating the beginning of a downtrend.

Other factors to consider

The examples given so far have taken days into account, but this is not a necessary requirement for moving averages. For day trading it might be interesting to look at how an asset has moved in the past two or three hours, not two or three months. Different time frames can be entered into the equations used to calculate moving averages, and as long as these intervals are consistent with the trading strategy, the data can be useful.

Since MAs are lagging indicators that consider previous price movements, signals are often produced too late. For example, a bullish crossover might suggest a buying opportunity, but it only happens after a significant price increase. This means that, even if the upward trend continues, a potential gain could be lost in the period between the price increase and the crossover signal. Or worse still, a fake golden cross signal could lead the trader to buy the local top just before a price drop (these fake buy signals are often referred to as a bull trap). The only way to avoid these mistakes is to use moving averages in combination with other indicators.

Moving averages are among the most valid and widespread indicators. The ability to analyze market trends by evaluating the available data offers an excellent understanding of market movements. However, keep in mind that moving average and crossover signals should not be used alone and it is always safer to combine several technical analysis indicators to avoid fake signals.

Chapter 7 - Golden Cross and Death Cross

Now that we have discussed the difference between simple moving averages and exponential moving averages, it is time to discover how you can use them to craft a performing trading strategy.

The Golden Cross

A golden cross, also called golden crossover, is a chart pattern involving a short-term moving average that crosses a long-term moving average to the upside. Typically, the 50-day moving average is used as the short-term mean and the 200-day moving average as the long-term mean. However, this is not the only way to think about the golden cross.

Typically, a golden cross occurs in three stages:

- The short-term moving average sits below the long-term moving average during a downtrend.
- The trend reverses, and the short-term moving average crosses the long-term moving average to the upside.

- An uptrend begins where the short-term moving average stays above the long-term moving average.

In many cases, a golden cross can be considered a bullish signal. Why? Well, the idea is simple. We know that a moving average measures the average price of an asset over a certain period of time. In this sense, when a short-term moving average is below a long-term moving average, it means that the short-term price movements are bearish relative to the long-term price movements.

Now, what happens when the short-term average crosses the long-term average to the upside? The short-term average price exceeds the long-term average price. This indicates a potential change of direction in the market trend, which is why a golden cross is considered bullish.

In the conventional interpretation, a golden cross involves the 50-day moving average that crosses the 200-day moving average to the upside. However, the general idea behind the golden cross is that a short-term moving average crosses a long-term moving average to the upside. In this sense, we can also have golden crosses on other time frames (15 minutes, 1 hour, 4 hours, etc.). However, signals over longer intervals tend to be more reliable than signals over shorter intervals.

So far, we have considered a golden cross with what we call a simple moving average (SMA). However, exponential moving averages can also be used to look for bullish or bearish crosses, including the golden cross. As the exponential moving averages react faster to recent price movements, the crossover signals they produce may be less reliable and present more false signals. Despite this, exponential moving average crosses are popular with traders as a tool for identifying trend reversals.

The Death Cross

Basically, a death cross is the opposite of a golden cross. It is a chart pattern where a short term moving average crosses down a long term moving average to the downside. For example, when the 50-day moving average crosses down the 200-day moving average to the downside. Therefore, a death cross is usually considered a bearish signal.

Typically, a death cross occurs in three stages:

- The short-term moving average sits above the long-term moving average during an uptrend.
- The trend reverses, and the short-term moving average crosses down the long-term moving average.

- A downtrend begins where the short-term moving average stays below the long-term moving average.

Now that we know the golden cross, it's pretty easy to understand why a death cross is a bearish signal. The short-term average crosses the long-term average downwards, indicating a bearish outlook on the market.

The death cross has provided a bearish signal before economic recessions in history, such as in 1929 or 2008. However, it could also provide false signals, as it did in 2016.

Golden Cross vs. Death Cross

We've talked about both, so the difference between the two isn't hard to understand. They are essentially the exact opposite of each other. The golden cross can be considered as a bullish signal, while the death cross is a bearish signal.

Both can be confirmed by high trading volume. Some technical analysts may also check other technical indicators in the context of a cross. Common examples include the Moving Average Convergence Divergence (MACD) and the Relative Strength Index (RSI).

It is also important to remember that moving averages are lagging indicators and have no predictive power. This means that both crosses will typically provide strong confirmation of a trend reversal when this has already occurred - they will not signal a reversal that is still in progress.

Golden Cross, Death Cross, and trading

The basic idea behind these patterns is pretty clear. If you know how traders use the MACD indicator, you will easily understand how to use crossover signals.

As for conventional golden cross and death cross, we generally analyze the daily chart. So, a simple strategy would be to buy at a golden cross and sell at a death cross. Indeed, this strategy would have had moderate success on Bitcoin in recent years - despite several false signals along the way. Hence, blindly following a signal is not usually the best strategy. Therefore, you may want to consider other factors in your market analysis technique.

The crossover strategy mentioned above is based on moving average crossings on daily charts. What about the other time frames? Golden crosses and death crosses happen the same way, and traders can take advantage of them.

However, as with most chart analysis techniques, signals over longer ranges are stronger than signals over shorter ranges. A golden cross could occur on the weekly time frame, just as you watch a death cross on the hourly chart. For this reason, it is always useful to observe the general picture of the chart, taking into account different time frames.

In trading with golden crosses and death crosses, many traders will also observe the trading volume. As with other chart patterns, volume can be a valid confirmation tool. For instance, when a spike in volume accompanies a crossover signal, many traders will be more confident in the validity of the signal.

After a golden cross, the long-term moving average could be seen as a potential support area. Conversely, after a death cross, it can be considered as a potential resistance area.

Crossover signals can also be compared to other technical indicators to look for confluences. Confluence traders combine different signals and indicators into a single trading strategy in an effort to make the signals more reliable. Our experience tells us that this is the best method to analyze a chart and we highly recommend you take advantage of all the indicators and chart patterns described in this book.

Chapter 8 - The MACD

The Moving Average Convergence Divergence (MACD) indicator is an oscillator widely used by traders for technical analysis. The MACD is a tool that applies moving averages to determine the momentum of a stock, a cryptocurrency or another asset.

Developed by Gerald Appel in the late 1970s, the Moving Average Convergence Divergence indicator tracks price events that have already occurred and falls into the category of lagging indicators (which provide signals based on past prices or data). The MACD can be useful for determining the momentum of the market and possible price trends and is used by many traders to identify potential entry and exit points.

How MACD works

The MACD indicator is generated by making the difference between two exponential moving averages to create the main line (MACD line), which is then used to calculate another exponential moving average that represents the signal line.

Added to this is the MACD histogram, calculated based on the differences between these two lines. The histogram, together with the other lines, fluctuates above and below a central line, also known as the zero line. Therefore, the MACD indicator consists of three elements that move around the zero line:

- The MACD line. It helps determine upward or downward impulses (market trends). It is calculated from the difference between two exponential moving averages.
- The signal line. It is a MACD line exponential moving average (typically a 9 period exponential moving average). The combined analysis of the signal line with the MACD line can be useful for identifying potential inversions or points of entry or exit.
- The histogram. It is a graphic representation of the divergence and convergence between the MACD line and the signal line. In other words, the histogram is calculated based on the differences between the two lines.

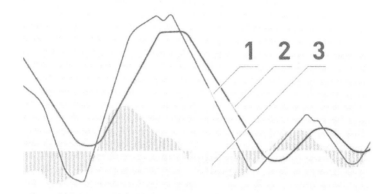

The MACD line

Typically, exponential moving averages are measured according to the closing prices of an asset, and the periods used to calculate the two EMAs are usually set at 12 periods (faster) and 26 periods (slower). The period can be configured in several ways (minutes, hours, days, weeks, months), but in this chapter we will focus on daily settings. However, the MACD indicator can be customized to suit different trading strategies.

Assuming standard time frames, the MACD line is calculated by subtracting the 26-day EMA from the 12-day EMA.

MACD line = 12d EMA - 26d EMA

As noted above, the MACD line fluctuates above and below the zero line, and when this occurs a zero crossing happens, signaling to traders when the 12-day and 26-day exponential moving averages are changing their relative positions.

The signal line

Normally, the signal line is calculated from a 9-day exponential moving average of the MACD line and provides more information on its previous movements.

Signal line = 9d EMA of the MACD line

While it is not always accurate, when the MACD line and the signal line cross could be seen as a trend reversal signal, especially when this occurs at the bottom of the MACD chart.

The MACD histogram

The histogram is simply a visual record of the relative movements of the MACD line and the signal line. It is calculated by subtracting one from the other:

MACD histogram = MACD line - signal line

However, instead of adding a third line, the histogram is composed of a candle chart, making it visually easier to examine and interpret. The candles in the histogram have nothing to do with the trading volume of the asset.

MACD settings

As already mentioned, the standard settings for MACD are based on 12, 26 and 9 period EMAs - hence MACD (12, 26, 9). However, some analysts change the periods to create a more sensitive indicator. For example, the MACD (5, 35, 5) is a pattern often used in traditional financial markets on longer time frames, such as weekly or monthly charts.

It is important to emphasize that due to the high volatility of the cryptocurrency markets, increasing the sensitivity of the MACD indicator can be risky as it is likely to result in a greater number of false signals and misleading information.

How to read MACD charts

As the name suggests, the Moving Average Convergence Divergence indicator tracks the relationships between moving averages, and the correlation between the two lines which can be described as convergent or divergent. The correlation is converging when the lines approach each other and diverging when they move apart.

The relevant signals of the MACD indicator concern the so-called crossings, which occur when the MACD line crosses the zero line up or down (zero crossing), or the signal line (signal line crossing).

Remember that both zero crossings and signal line crossings can occur multiple times, producing many false and deceptive signals - especially when dealing with volatile assets, such as cryptocurrencies. Consequently, it is not wise to rely on the MACD indicator alone.

Zero crossing

Zero crossings occur when the MACD line crosses the zero line up or down. When it gets to the top, the positive MACD value indicates that the 12-day EMA is greater than the 26-day EMA.

Conversely, a negative MACD is recorded when the MACD line reaches the bottom of the chart, signaling that the 26-day average is higher than the 12-day one. In other words, a positive MACD line suggests a stronger upward momentum, while a negative one may indicate a stronger downward momentum.

Crossing of the signal line

When the MACD line crosses the signal line going up, traders identify a potential buying opportunity (entry point). Conversely, when the MACD line crosses the signal line downwards, traders tend to consider a sales opportunity (exit point).

While crossing signs can be useful, they are not always reliable. It is important to consider at which point on the chart they occur to minimize the risks. For example, if the crossing suggests a buy but the MACD line is below the central line, market conditions could still be considered bearish. Conversely, if a signal line crossing indicates a potential selling point but the MACD line is positive (above the zero line), market conditions are likely still bullish. In this scenario, following the sell signal can carry greater risk (considering the more general trend).

Divergences between MACD and price

Together with the zero and signal line crossings, the MACD indicator can also provide information through divergences between the MACD chart and the asset prices.

For example, if the price of a cryptocurrency reaches a higher high while the MACD marks a lower high, we have a bearish divergence, indicating that despite the price increase, the upward momentum (buying pressure) has become weaker. Bearish divergences are usually interpreted as selling opportunities as they tend to precede price reversals.

On the contrary, if the MACD line marks a higher low that aligns with a lower low on the price chart, a bullish divergence is formed, suggesting that despite the price drop, the buying pressure is stronger. Bullish divergences tend to precede trend reversals, potentially indicating a short-term bottom (from a downtrend to an uptrend).

The MACD is often used in combination with the RSI to identify trend reversals and divergences.

Chapter 9 - Stochastic RSI

The Stochastic RSI, or StochRSI, is a technical analysis indicator used to determine whether an asset is overbought or oversold, as well as identifying current market trends. As the name suggests, the StochRSI is a derivative of the standard Relative Strength Index (RSI), and as such is considered an indicator of an indicator.

The StochRSI was first described in 1994, in the book The New Technical Trader by Stanley Kroll and Tushar Chande. It is often used by stock traders, but can also be applied to other trading contexts, such as the forex and cryptocurrency markets.

How the StochRSI works

The StochRSI indicator is generated from the normal RSI by applying the Stochastic Oscillator formula. The result is a numerical evaluation that oscillates around a midline (0.5), within a range of 0-1. However, there are modified versions of the StochRSI indicator that multiply the results by 100, so the values are between 0 and 100 instead of 0 and 1. Oftentimes you can also see a 3-day simple moving average (SMA) along with the StochRSI line, with the signal line function and the aim of reducing the risk of false signals.

The standard formula for the Stochastic Oscillator considers the closing price of an asset together with its highest and lowest points within a given period. However, when the formula is used to calculate the StochRSI, it is directly applied to the RSI data and prices are not considered.

Stoch RSI = (Current RSI - Lowest RSI) / (Highest RSI - Lowest RSI)

As for the standard RSI, the most common interval used for the StochRSI is 14 periods. The 14 periods involved in the StochRSI calculation are based on the timeframe of the chart. So while a daily time frame chart considers the last 14 days, an hourly time frame chart generates the StochRSI based on the last 14 hours.

Periods can be set for days, hours or even minutes, and their use varies greatly from trader to trader (depending on profile and strategy). The number of periods can also be increased or decreased to identify longer or shorter term trends. A 20-period setting is another rather popular option for the StochRSI indicator.

As already mentioned, some StochRSI models assign values ranging from 0 to 100 instead of 0 to 1. In these cases, the midline is found at 50 instead of 0.5. Consequently, the overbought signal that is typically indicated at 0.8 is presented at 80, and the oversold signal is presented at 20 instead of 0.2. Models with a 0-100 setting may appear slightly different, but the practical interpretation remains essentially the same.

Using the StochRSI

The StochRSI indicator takes on its greatest importance near the upper and lower limits of its range. Consequently, the primary use of the indicator is to identify potential entry and exit points, as well as trend reversals. Thus, a signal of 0.2 or lower indicates that an asset is likely oversold, while a signal of 0.8 or higher suggests that it is likely overbought.

Additionally, signals closer to the midline can provide useful information regarding market trends. For example, when the midline acts as support and the StochRSI lines regularly move above the 0.5 point, it could suggest a continuation of an uptrend - especially if the lines start moving towards 0.8.

Likewise, signals regularly below 0.5 and moving towards 0.2 indicate a bearish trend.

StochRSI vs. RSI

Both the StochRSI and the RSI are oscillator indicators, which allow traders to identify potential overbought and oversold conditions, as well as possible reversal points. In short, the standard RSI is a model used to monitor how quickly and to what extent the prices of an asset change in relation to a certain time frame.

However, compared to the Stochastic RSI, the standard RSI is a relatively slow indicator that produces a limited number of signals. The application of the Stochastic Oscillator formula to the regular RSI has allowed the creation of the StochRSI as an indicator with greater sensitivity. As a result, the number of signals it produces is much higher, giving traders more opportunities to identify market trends and potential buy or sell points.

In other words, the StochRSI is a rather volatile indicator, and while this makes it a more sensitive technical analysis instrument that can help traders with more signals, it also gives it a more risky aspect as it often generates false signals. As already mentioned, applying simple moving averages is a common method to reduce the risks associated with these false signals and, in many cases, a 3-day simple moving average is already included as the default setting for the StochRSI indicator.

Chapter 10 - Bollinger Bands

The Bollinger Bands were created in the early 1980s by trader and financial analyst John Bollinger. Bollinger Bands are widely used as a tool for technical analysis. Essentially, it is an oscillator that indicates whether the market has high or low volatility and whether it is overbought or oversold.

The central idea behind the Bollinger Bands indicator is to highlight how prices are dispersed around an average value. More precisely, the indicator is composed of an upper band, a lower band and an intermediate line representing the moving average (also called the average band). The two outer bands react to the price action, expanding when volatility is high (moving away from the midline) and contracting when volatility is low (approaching the midline).

The formula for Bollinger Bands

The standard formula for Bollinger Bands sets the center line as a 20-day simple moving average, while the upper and lower bands are calculated based on market volatility in relation to the simple moving average. This relationship is called standard deviation. The standard settings for the Bollinger Bands indicator look like this:

- Midline: 20-day simple moving average
- Upper band: 20-day simple moving average + (20-day standard deviation x2)
- Lower band: 20-day simple moving average - (20-day standard deviation x2)

The standard Bollinger Bands settings observe a period of 20 days and fix the outer bands at a distance of two standard deviations from the central line. In this way it is possible to ensure that at least 85% of the price moves are within these two bands, but the settings can be changed according to different needs and trading strategies.

Bollinger Bands and trading

Bollinger Bands are widely used in traditional financial markets, but can also be used for cryptocurrency trading. Of course, there are several ways to use and interpret the Bollinger Bands indicator, but in general it is better to avoid using the Bollinger Bands as an independent tool and not consider it an indicator of buy/sell opportunities. Instead, Bollinger Bands should be used in conjunction with other technical indicators, like those we analyzed in previous chapters.

Keeping this in mind, let's take a look at how to potentially interpret the data provided by the Bollinger Bands indicator.

If the price makes its way up above the moving average and breaks out of the upper band, it is probably fair to assume that the market is in an overbought condition. Or, if the price hits the upper band several times, it could indicate a significant resistance level.

Conversely, if the price of a certain asset falls significantly and breaks or hits the lower band several times, the market is likely to be oversold or have found a strong support level. As a result, traders can use Bollinger Bands to define buy or sell targets or to get an overview of the previous points where the market has presented overbought and oversold conditions.

Furthermore, the expansion and contraction of the Bollinger Bands could be useful in predicting periods of high or low volatility. The bands can move away from the average line when the asset price becomes more volatile or approach it when the price becomes less volatile.

Hence, Bollinger Bands are best suited for short-term trading as a method of analyzing market volatility and trying to predict upcoming movements. Some traders believe that when the bands are too far apart, the current market trend could be close to a period of consolidation or a reversal. Conversely, when the bands get too tight, traders tend to assume that the market is preparing for an explosive move.

When the price moves sideways, the Bollinger Bands tend to tighten towards the moving average line. Usually, low volatility and tight levels of deviation precede large and explosive moves, which tend to occur as volatility begins to rise again.

Bollinger Bands vs Keltner Channels

Unlike Bollinger Bands, which are based on simple moving averages and standard deviations, the modern version of the Keltner Channels indicator uses the Average True Range to determine the channel width around an exponential moving average of 20 days. Hence, the Keltner Canal formula is the following:

- Midline: 20-day exponential moving average

- Upper channel line: 20-day exponential moving average + (10-day Average True Range x2)
- Lower band: 20-day exponential moving average - (10-day Average True Range x2)

Generally, the Keltner Channels indicator tends to be narrower than the Bollinger Bands. Consequently, it may be better suited than Bollinger Bands to recognize trend reversals and overbought/oversold conditions more clearly and noticeably. Furthermore, the Keltner Channels indicator provides the overbought/oversold signal usually before the Bollinger Bands.

Conversely, Bollinger Bands tend to better represent market volatility as the expansion and contraction movements are broader and more explicit when compared to the Keltner Channels. In addition to this, thanks to the use of standard deviations, the Bollinger Bands indicator is less likely to provide incorrect signals, as its width is greater and, therefore, more difficult to overcome.

Between Bollinger Bands and Keltner Channels, Bollinger Bands are used much more frequently. However, both are good indicators - especially for short-term setups - and can also be used together to provide even more reliable signals.

Chapter 11 - Technical Analysis and Bitcoin Market Cycles

Market psychology is the concept that the movements of a market reflect (or are influenced by) the emotional state of its participants. It is one of the main themes of behavioral economics - an interdisciplinary field that examines the various factors that precede economic decisions.

Many believe that emotions are the main driving force behind changes in financial markets, and that the general fluctuating sentiment of investors creates so-called psychological market cycles.

In short, market sentiment is the general feeling that investors and traders have about movements in the price of an asset. When market sentiment is positive, and prices are continuously rising, we are facing a bullish trend (often referred to as a bull market). The opposite is called the bear market, when there is a continuous decline in prices. Hence, sentiment is made up of the individual views and feelings of all traders and investors within a financial market. From another point of view, it is an average of the general feelings of market participants.

However, as with any group of people, there is not a completely dominant opinion. According to market psychology theories, the price of an asset tends to change constantly in reaction to general market sentiment - which is also dynamic. Otherwise, it would be much more difficult to conclude a successful transaction.

In practice, when the market is growing, it is likely due to a better attitude and greater confidence among traders. Positive market sentiment causes demand to rise and supply to fall. In turn, the higher demand could cause an even stronger attitude. Likewise, a strong downward trend tends to create negative sentiment which reduces demand and increases available supply.

Emotions in a bullish trend

All markets go through cycles of expansion and contraction. When a market is in an expansion phase (a bull market), there is a climate of optimism, conviction and greed. Typically, these are the main emotions that lead to strong buying activity.

It is quite common to see some kind of cyclical or retroactive effect during market cycles. For example, the sentiment becomes more positive as prices rise, which makes the sentiment even more positive, pushing the market higher and higher.

Sometimes, a strong sense of greed and conviction pervades the market in such a way that a financial bubble can form. In such a scenario, many investors become irrational, losing sight of true value and buying an asset only by virtue of the belief that the market will continue to rise. They become greedy and too excited by the market momentum, hoping to make a profit. When the price has expanded too high, a local spike is created. In general, this is considered to be the point of maximum financial risk.

In some cases, the market will experience sideways movement for a while as assets are gradually sold. This interval is also known as the distribution phase. However, some cycles do not have a clear distribution phase, and the bearish trend begins soon after the peak is reached.

Emotions in a bearish trend

When the market starts to turn in the opposite direction, the euphoric state can quickly turn into carelessness as many traders refuse to believe that the uptrend is over. As prices continue to drop, market sentiment quickly moves to the negative side. It often includes feelings of anxiety, rejection and panic.

In this context, we could describe anxiety as the moment when investors start wondering why the price is falling, which soon leads to the rejection phase. The period of rejection is marked by a sense of denial. Many investors insist on holding their positions at a loss, either because "it is too late to sell" or because they want to believe that "the market will recover soon".

However, as prices drop further, the sales surge becomes stronger. At this point, fear and panic often lead to what we call market capitulation (when holders give up and sell their assets near the local lows).

Eventually, the bearish trend stops as volatility decreases and the market stabilizes. Typically, the market experiences sideways movements before feelings of hope and optimism start to build up again. This lateral period is also known as the accumulation phase.

Investors, traders and market psychology

Assuming the market psychology theory is valid, understanding it could help a trader open and close positions at more favorable times. The general market attitude is counterproductive: the moment of greatest financial opportunity (for a buyer) usually comes when the majority have lost hope, and the prices are very low. Conversely, the time of greatest financial risk often comes when the majority of market participants are excited and overconfident.

Hence, some traders and investors try to read the sentiment of a market to identify the various stages of its psychological cycles. Ideally, they would use this information to buy when they see panic (lower prices) and sell when they see greed (higher prices). However, in practice, recognizing these optimal points is no easy feat. What appears to be the local bottom (support) may not hold up, leading to even lower prices.

Technical analysis and market psychology

It is easy to look back at the market cycles and recognize how the general psychology has changed. Analyzing previous data makes it clear which actions and decisions would have been the most profitable.

However, it is much more difficult to understand how the market is changing in real time - and even more difficult to predict what will happen next. Many investors use technical analysis to try to anticipate where the market might move.

In a sense, we could say that TA indicators are tools that can be used when trying to assess the psychological state of the market. For example, the Relative Strength Index (RSI) indicator could suggest when an asset is overbought due to strong positive market sentiment (e.g., excess greed).

MACD is another example of an indicator that could be used to identify the different psychological phases of a market cycle. In short, the relationship between its lines could indicate when market momentum is changing (e.g., the buying force is weakening). We have discussed some basic technical analysis strategies in a previous chapter.

Bitcoin and market psychology

The 2017 Bitcoin bull market is a clear example of how market psychology affects prices and vice versa. From January to December, Bitcoin jumped from around $900 to the all-time high of $20,000. On the way up, market sentiment became increasingly positive. Thousands of new investors joined, caught up in the bull market excitement. FOMO, excessive optimism and greed quickly pushed prices up - until they did not.

The turnaround began to take shape in late 2017 and early 2018. The subsequent correction left many of the late market participants with significant losses. However, even when the bearish trend had already established itself, the false confidence and carelessness prompted many people to persist in their HODLing.

A few months later, market sentiment turned very negative as investor confidence hit a low. Fear, uncertainty, doubt and panic have led many of those who bought near the high to sell near the low, realizing large losses. Some people became disillusioned with Bitcoin, even though the technology was essentially the same and there were not fundamental changes.

Cognitive distortions

Cognitive distortions are common thought patterns that often lead humans to make irrational decisions. These patterns can affect both individual traders and the market as a whole. Some common examples are the following.

- **Confirmation bias**. This is the tendency to overestimate information that confirms our beliefs, ignoring or rejecting information that goes against them. For example, investors in a bull market might focus more on positive news, ignoring bad news or signs that a turnaround is approaching.

- **Loss aversion**. This is the common tendency of humans to fear losses more than they enjoy profits, even if the profit is similar or greater. In other words, the pain of a loss is generally more intense than the joy of a gain. This could lead to traders missing out on good opportunities or panicking and selling during periods of market capitulation.

- **Endowment effect**. This is the tendency in people to overestimate things they own, simply because they own them. For example, an investor who owns cryptocurrencies is more likely to be more convinced of its value than a no-coiner is.

Most traders and investors believe that psychology has an impact on prices and market cycles. While the psychological market cycles are well known, they are not always easy to deal with. From Dutch Tulipomania in the 1600s to the dotcom bubble in the 1990s, even experienced traders have had a hard time separating their attitude from general market sentiment. Investors are faced with the difficult task of understanding not only the psychology of the market but also their own psychology and the ways in which it affects their decision-making process. Our suggestion is simple to understand but difficult to follow: buy when others are fearful and sell when others are greedy.

Chapter 12 - Trend Lines

In the previous chapter we have discussed the different emotions in a bullish and a bearish trend. But how do you determine whether the market is bullish or bearish? Well, you might be tempted to answer that it is quite obvious: when price rises the market is bullish, when it falls the market is bearish.

While this practical definition might be true, we need a clear indicator that tells us the direction of the market. Trend lines do exactly this and the next few pages are going to tell you everything you need to know about them.

In the context of cryptocurrency markets, trend lines are diagonal lines drawn on charts. They link specific points, allowing analysts and traders to more easily visualize price movements and identify market trends. Trend lines are considered to be one of the most basic tools in technical analysis.

Trend lines are widely used in the equity, forex, derivatives and cryptocurrency markets. Essentially, trend lines act as support and resistance levels but are formed by diagonals instead of horizontal lines. For this reason, they can have a positive or negative inclination. In general, the greater the slope of the line, the stronger the trend.

We can divide the trend lines into two basic categories: bullish (uptrend line) and bearish (downtrend line). As the name suggests, a bullish line is drawn from a lower point to a higher point on the chart. It connects two or more points as shown in the image below.

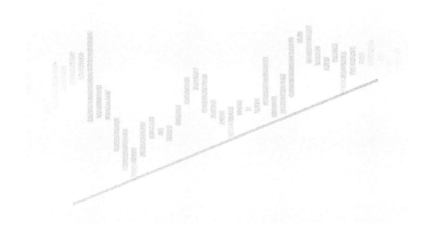

Conversely, a bearish line is drawn from a higher to a lower position in the chart. It connects two or more points of maximum.

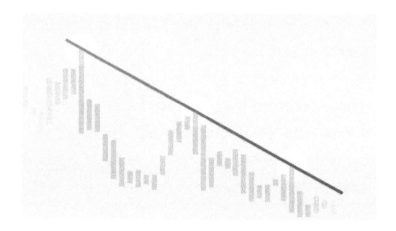

In summary, the difference between these two types of lines is the selection of the points used to draw them. In an uptrend, the lines are drawn using the lowest points in the chart (minimum points rising between them). Instead, a bearish trend line is drawn using the highest values (maximum points decreasing between them).

How to use trend lines

Based on the highs and lows of a chart, the trend lines indicate where the price has tried to oppose the prevailing trend. The line can then be extended to try to predict important levels in the future. As long as the trend line is not broken, it is considered valid.

While trend lines can be used on any type of data chart, they are generally based on market prices. This means that they can also provide information on market supply and demand. Of course, bullish trend lines indicate increasing purchasing power (demand is greater than supply). Bearish trend lines are associated with substantial price drops, suggesting the opposite (supply is greater than demand).

However, trading volume should also be considered in these analysis. For example, if the price is rising, but the volume is decreasing or is relatively low, it could give a false impression of higher demand.

As already mentioned, trend lines are used to identify support and resistance levels, two basic but very important concepts of technical analysis. A bullish line shows support levels below which the price is unlikely to drop. Conversely, the bearish line highlights resistance levels above which the price is unlikely to rise.

In other words, the market trend can be considered invalid when support and resistance levels are broken. In many cases, when these key levels fail to maintain the trend, the market tends to change direction.

Draw valid trend lines

While trend lines can technically connect any two points in a chart, most analysts agree that using three or more points is what makes a trend line valid. In some cases, the first two points can be used to define a potential trend, and the third point (extended into the future) can be used to test its validity.

So when the price touches the trend line three or more times without breaking it, the trend can be considered valid. Testing the trend line several times suggests that the trend is not a mere coincidence caused by price fluctuations.

Scale settings

In addition to choosing enough points to create a valid trendline, it's important to consider the right settings when drawing a trend line. Among the most important chart settings are the scale settings.

In cryptocurrency charts, scale refers to how the change in price is displayed. The two best known scales are arithmetic and semi-logarithmic (semi-log). In an arithmetic chart, the change appears uniformly as the price moves up or down on the Y axis. Semi-log charts express changes in terms of percentages.

For example, a change in price from $5 to $10 would cover the same distance on an arithmetic chart as a change from $120 to $125 in a semi-log chart. However, the 100% increase ($5 to $10) would take up a much larger portion of the chart than the 4% increase caused by going from $120 to $125.

It is important to consider the scale settings when drawing trend lines. Each type of chart may show different highs and lows and, as a result, slightly different trend lines.

We highly recommend you use the logarithmic chart when drawing trend lines. In fact, our experience tells us that it offers much more accurate predictions of where price will bounce next.

Chapter 13 - Common Technical Analysis Mistakes

Even though the basic concepts of technical analysis are relatively simple to understand, it is a difficult art to master. When you're learning a new skill, it's natural to make mistakes. This can be especially damaging when it comes to trading or investing. If you are not careful and do not learn from your mistakes, you risk losing a significant portion of your capital. Learning from your mistakes is helpful, but avoiding them as much as possible is even better.

This chapter will introduce you to some of the most common mistakes in technical analysis. Let's get started!

Not cutting your losses

Let's start with a quote from the famous commodity trader Ed Seykota:

"The elements of good trading are: (1) cut your losses, (2) cut your losses, (3) cut your losses. If you follow these three rules you may have a chance."

This seems like a simple step, but it is always good to emphasize its importance. When it comes to trading and investing, protecting your capital should always be the number one priority.

The first steps in trading can be daunting. A solid approach to consider in the beginning is this: the first step is not to win, it is not to lose. For this reason it can be useful to start with smaller positions, or not to risk real funds. Binance Futures, for example, has a testnet where you can test your strategies before risking your funds. This way, you can protect your capital and only risk it when you are consistently producing good results.

Setting a stop-loss is simple and reasonable. Your operations should have an invalidation point, where you "bite the bullet" and accept that your idea was wrong. If you don't apply this mindset to trading, chances are you won't have much success in the long run. It only takes one trade that goes wrong to do serious damage to your portfolio, and you could find yourself in a losing streak, hoping that the market will recover. As you should know by now, hoping is not a trading strategy.

Overtrading

For an active trader, it is a common mistake to believe that they must always be in a trade. Trading involves a lot of analysis and a lot of patient waiting! With some trading strategies, you may have to wait a long time to get a reliable signal and open a position. Some traders open less than three positions per year and still produce excellent returns.

As this quote from trader Jesse Livermore, one of the pioneers of day trading, says:

> *"Money is made by waiting, not trading."*

Try not to get into a position for the sake of it. You don't always have to be in an operation. In fact, under certain market conditions, it is more profitable to do nothing and wait for an opportunity to arise. This way, you preserve your capital and are ready to use it when good trading opportunities arise again. It is important to remember that opportunities always come back, you just have to wait for them.

A similar trading mistake is an overemphasis on the lower time frames. Analysis performed on longer time frames will generally be more reliable than analysis performed on lower intervals. The latter will produce a lot of market noise and may tempt you to enter positions too often. While there are many successful scalpers and short-term traders, trading in lower ranges has a very bad risk / reward ratio. Being a risky trading strategy, it is certainly not recommended for beginners.

Revenge trading

It is quite common to see traders trying to recover a substantial loss immediately. This is called revenge trading. It doesn't matter if you want to be a technical analyst, day trader or swing trader - avoiding emotional decisions is key.

It's easy to stay calm when things are going well, or when you make small mistakes. But can you stay calm when things go completely wrong? Can you stick to your trading plan, even when everyone else is panicking?

Notice the word "analysis" in technical analysis. Of course, this implies an analytical approach to the markets, right? So why would you make emotional decisions in such a scenario? If you want to be among the best traders, you need to be able to stay calm even after the biggest mistakes. Avoid emotional decisions, and focus on maintaining a logical and analytical mindset.

Trading immediately after suffering a large loss tends to generate further losses. For this reason, some traders decide not to trade for a period of time following a large loss. This way, they can start from scratch and return to trading with a clear mind.

Being too stubborn to change your mind

If you want to become a successful trader, you should not be afraid to change your mind. Market conditions can change rapidly, and one thing is certain. They will continue to change. Your job as a trader is to recognize these changes and adapt to them. A strategy that works very well in one specific market context may not work in another scenario.

Legendary trader Paul Tudor Jones said a very interesting thing about this topic:

"Every day I think my position is wrong."

It is helpful to try to take the opposing side of your position to identify its potential weaknesses. This way, your investment theses and decisions can be more accurate.

Cognitive distortions

This brings us to another point: cognitive distortions. Biases can heavily affect your decision making process, cloud your judgment, and limit the range of possibilities you are able to consider. At least, make sure you understand the cognitive distortions that could affect your trading plans, so that you can mitigate their consequences more effectively.

Ignoring extreme market conditions

There are times when the predictive qualities of TA become less reliable. These can be black swan events or other types of extreme market conditions driven heavily by mass emotion and psychology. Ultimately, markets are driven by supply and demand, and there may be times when they are extremely unbalanced towards one of these two sides.

Let's take the Relative Strength Index (RSI) as an example. Typically, if the value is below 30, the analyzed asset can be considered oversold. Does this mean we have an immediate trading signal when the RSI drops below 30? Absolutely not! It just means that the momentum of the market is currently being dictated by the sellers side. In other words, it just indicates that sellers are stronger than buyers.

The RSI can reach extreme levels during extraordinary market conditions. It could even go to single digits. Even an extreme oversold reading may not mean a reversal is imminent.

Making blind decisions based on technical tools that reach extreme values can make you lose a lot of money. This is especially true during black swan events when price movements can be incredibly difficult to analyze. During periods of this kind, markets can continue in one direction or another, and no analytical tool will be able to stop them. For this reason it is always important to consider other factors as well, and not to rely on a single tool.

TA is a game of chance

Technical analysis does not deal with absolutes. It deals with probability. This means that whatever technical approach you are basing your strategies on, there is never a guarantee that the market will behave as you expect. Perhaps your analysis suggests a very high probability that the market will move up or down, but it's still not a certainty.

You need to take this factor into consideration when setting up your trading strategies. No matter how experienced you are, it is never a good idea to think that the market will follow your analysis. If you do, you will tend to open too large positions and bet too much on an outcome, risking a large financial loss. If you feel this is one of the mistakes you make, try to lower the size of your trading account.

Blindly following other traders

Constantly improving your skills is essential to mastering trading. This is especially true when it comes to trading in the cryptocurrency market. Indeed, the ever-changing market conditions make it a necessity. One of the best ways to learn is to follow technical analysts and experienced traders.

However, if you want to grow as a trader, you also need to find your strengths and build on them. You can consider them your advantage, the element that makes you different from other traders.

If you read a lot of interviews of successful traders, you will surely notice that they have very different strategies. In fact, a strategy that works perfectly for one trader may be considered completely unfeasible by another. There are endless ways to profit from the cryptocurrency market. You just have to find the one that best suits your personality and your trading style.

Getting into a position based on someone else's analysis might work a few times. However, if you blindly follow other traders without understanding the underlying context, it will undoubtedly not work in the long term. Of course, this doesn't mean you shouldn't follow and learn from others. The important thing is whether you agree with the idea and whether it fits into your trading system. You shouldn't follow other traders blindly, even if they are experienced and respected. This also means you should not subscribe to signal groups or other "mentorship" programs where you are told what trades to take. If you want to become a good trader, you have to understand that it is a lonely journey.

Conclusion

Congratulations on making it to the end of this book, we hope you found some useful information to take your cryptocurrency trading skills to the next level. By now, you should know that the world of cryptocurrency is extremely complicated and that there is a new "opportunity" every way you look. Please, do not get caught up in this shiny object syndrome. Our experience tells us that only by taking things seriously and having a proper plan you can develop your trading skills to the point that you can actually trade for a living. It will not happen by tomorrow, but if you stick to it and improve a bit every day, you will reach that goal sooner than you think.

Choose a trading strategy you want to master and study it in depth. After you have sufficient knowledge on what you are talking about, apply the other fundamental and technical analysis strategies we have discussed in this book. Analyze your results, improve your money management skills and become the master of your emotions.

As you can see, there are no shortcuts to success. Easy money does not exist; never has and never will. What exists is the possibility to start from zero and work your way up to become a professional trader. The journey might be difficult, but it is certainly worth it. We talk from experience.

To your success!

Charles Swing and *Masaru Nakamoto*

Bitcoin

Lightning Source UK Ltd.
Milton Keynes UK
UKHW020735260521
384399UK00001B/117